T0084717

IF EINSTEIN HAD BEEN A SURFER

Other titles of interest from St. Augustine's Press

IF EINSTEIN
HAD BEEN A SURFER

A Surfer, a Scientist, and a Philosopher
Discuss a "Universal Wave Theory" or
"Theory of Everything"

Peter Kreeft

ST. AUGUSTINE'S PRESS
South Bend, Indiana
2009

Manufactured in the United States of America.

1 2 3 4 5 6   15 14 13 12 11 10 09

Library of Congress Cataloging in Publication Data
Kreeft, Peter.
If Einstein had been a surfer: a surfer, a scientist,
and a philosopher discuss a "universal wave theory"
or "theory of everything" / Peter Kreeft.
p. cm.
ISBN-13: 978-1-58731-378-3 (hardcover: alk. paper)
ISBN-10: 1-58731-378-2 (hardcover: alk. paper)
1. Philosophy and science. I. Title.
B67.K73 2009
100 – dc22   2009012131

∞ *The paper used in this publication meets the minimum
requirements of the American National Standard for
Information Sciences – Permanence of Paper for Printed
Materials, ANSI Z39.48-1984.*

St. Augustine's Press
www.staugustine.net

Contents

Preface
What This Strange Book Is About

EINSTEIN NEVER FOUND IT. He called it the "Unified Field Theory." Later scientists, less modestly, called it the "Theory of Everything." But they did not find it either. The unicorn has never been captured.

Nor will it be captured here. This book is not so mad as to claim that. These are just some notes *toward* a "Theory of Everything." This is not the golden castle, or even the door to the castle, or even the road to the door to the castle. In fact, maybe it's not even a map to the road to the door to the castle. But it might be a map to the map.

Does it sound "flaky"? So does the universe. Einstein said, "Once you can accept the universe as matter expanding into nothing that is something, wearing stripes with plaid comes easy." Niels Bohr said of quantum theory, "If you're not shocked by it, you don't understand it." That's true of *everything*. (Think that through, please.)

This book may sound "flaky," but it is not "New Age" flakiness. It is the flakiness of the real universe, as known by modern science and as critiqued by hard-headed philosophy. One of its three authors is a physicist and another is a philosopher. The third is a psychologist – and a surfer. And *that* flakiness just might possibly be the catalyst we need to get closer to a Theory of Everything, because it just might possibly correspond to the "flakiness" of the real universe. Thus the title of the book.

* * * * *

In 2007, newspapers around the world ran a story about a scientist/mathematician/engineer in California who may have come up with the formula for the "Unified Field Theory" after all. He was a surfer.

This is not a joke. This is a fact. Here is the text, from Roger Highfield, Science Editor of the *Telegraph,* the U.K. online publication:

Surfer dude stuns physicists with the theory of everything.

An impoverished surfer has drawn up a new theory of the universe, seen by some as the Holy Grail of physics, which has received rave reviews from scientists. Garrett Lisi, 39, has a doctorate but no university affiliation and spends most of the year surfing in Hawaii. . . .

Lisi's inspiration lies in the most elegant and intricate shape known to mathematicians, called E8 – a complex, eight-dimensional mathematical pattern with 248 points first found in 1887, but only fully understood by mathematicians this year after work-ings that, if written out in tiny print, would cover an area the size of Manhattan.

That fact the Lisi was a surfer *seemed* to be acci-dental; but was it? Surfing was not included in any way in his theory, as an intellectual object – of course. And he did not credit his surfing in any way with having led him to his theory, as an intellectual method – of course. Or is that "of course" perhaps off course rather than on course?

If Einstein had been a surfer, might he have found the Theory of Everything?

* * * * *

The origin of this book is not any laughably embar-rassing attempt on my part to go beyond Einstein. That would be like trying to go beyond St. Michael the Archangel. Its origin is simply my eavesdropping on three very unusual friends of mine who had a series of conversations about exactly this issue: about the Theory of Everything, about the relation between science, philosophy, and common sense, and about surfing as a kind of catalyst to this reac-tion, or a key to this lock, or a clue to this puzzle, or a matchmaker for this relationship.

Evan Jellema is a scientist with philosophical and theological interests. He is square, pale, Dutch, tall, skinny, red-haired, clumsy, friendly, and absent-minded. He also has a degree in theology from a prestigious Protestant seminary.

'Isa Ben Adam is a philosopher and a polymath with scientific interests. He is a Palestinian Muslim who emigrated to America when he was five. Though he says he is not a Sufi, he reads and admires the Sufis. He insists that he is *not* a mystic, however. He is very bright, very blunt, and very basic.

Libby (Liberty) Rawls is a surfer and a poet, among many other things. She is a sassy, classy Black lady who has been a private detective and a freelance journalist, and is now a psychiatric social worker.

So this book should be of interest to three kinds of people: scientists (including amateur scientists), philosophers (including amateur philosophers), and surfer-poets. (*All* genuine surfers and all genuine poets are amateurs, which means "lovers.")

The conversation is a highly-edited, spliced-together version of numerous conversations among these three friends that I tape-recorded. The original tapes were messier and longer. Any defects in this book should be traced to me, and any worthwhile insights to Evan, 'Isa and Libby.

This is my third book of conversations that include these characters. (The other two were *A Refutation of Moral Relativism* and *Islamic Dialogs*.) It does not matter whether the characters are real or fictional, or to what extent. The *what* is far more important than the *who*. As Thomas Aquinas said, "the study of philosophy is not the study of what men have said but of what is true." Or as Buddha said, "look not to me, look to my dharma [teaching]."

Conversation 1: Where's the formula?

Evan: I asked you two to this series of conversations for a very selfish reason. As you know, I'm fascinated with the "Theory of Everything" that scientists have been looking for ever since Einstein. And my hunch is that if we're going to find it we need something more than just more scientists, or even better scientists. My hunch is that we need philosophers too – and that's where you come in, 'Isa – and even someone like you, Libby, someone with the unusual combination of psychology and street smarts and a streak of mysticism.

Libby: Sorry to disappoint you, Evan, but the only mystical experience I ever had was on the lip of a wave.

Evan: That's what I meant, Libby.

Libby: You gotta be kidding. You think you're going to learn something about the Theory of Everything from me because I'm a surfer girl?

Evan: Maybe.

Libby: You mean you're thinking that maybe you have to forget all about logic for a while?

Evan: No, just the opposite. I think it's totally logical to ask for your input. You see, it's a three-premise syllogism:

First, the Theory of Everything is about energy, because that's what everything in the universe is.

And second, all forms of energy come in waves.

And third, you know a wave of water in a more intimate way than any of us know a wave of anything else.

So . . .

Libby: OK, I'm *in,* but whatever I can tell you, there's no way you're gonna reduce it to a formula.

'Isa: She's right, Evan. And that's why I have to confess that I'm skeptical. Essential to any theory in the physical sciences is quantification and, therefore, a mathematical formula. Isn't that true?

Evan: Yes.

'Isa: Well, where is your formula? Where are even your preliminary formulas,

Why a surfer is needed for a Theory of Everything

Why a formula is necessary

your partial formulas? Where are even your guesses about formulas?

Evan: I have none.

'Isa: I rest my case.

Evan: But instead of a formula I have a compelling reason for the absence of one.

'Isa: I'm listening.

Libby: So am I.

Evan: I don't think there can *be* a formula for the Theory of Everything, because a "Theory *of Everything*" must be a theory also *of science and its formulas.* Therefore it has to be more overarching, more universal, than any formula. It's *about* formulas, and what can be put into formulas, and it's also about what *can't* be put into formulas. It has to overarch and interface and relate both: the formulable and the unformulable, the quantitative and the non-quantitative.

Why a formula is impossible

Libby: And doesn't it have to include the minds that make the formulas too?

'Isa (ignoring Libby): Isn't there something like that in physics already, Evan?

Evan: What are you thinking of?

'Isa: At one level, so to speak, there's quantum physics – a strange, invisible level that's been unearthed only in the

The two physical levels

last century. And at another level there's the ordinary space-time continuum. In the continuum, energy comes in waves, but on the quantum level it manifests as quantum particles or quanta of energy – isn't that right?

Evan: Well, sort of.

'Isa: So a Theory of Everything would unify the two levels somehow.

The four physical forces

Evan: Yes. And it also would unify the four fundamental forces of the universe: gravity, electromagnetism, the weak nuclear force, and the strong nuclear force.

Libby: Can I put it in psychological terms?

'Isa: I doubt it. But let's hear you try.

The two psychological levels

Libby: Maybe the quantum level in physics is something like the unconscious level in psychology. It works by different rules, and it escapes the laws of the ordinary level, and yet it causes or conditions the ordinary level. That's what the unconscious does. Isn't that what the stuff scientists talk about in quantum physics does too?

Evan: Again, I have to say "sort of." Yes, it's at least a meaningful analogy.

'Isa: Well, that means that to have a truly universal Theory of Everything, you would have to unify the two levels physically – the quantum level and the ordinary level – just as a truly universal theory in psychology has to unify the conscious and the unconscious levels.

Libby: And it would also have to unify the two *areas* that have ordinary levels and deeper levels – I mean the physical and the mental.

'Isa: So it would unify four things: ordinary physics, quantum physics, ordinary consciousness, and the unconscious.

The four things a Theory of Everything must unify

Evan: Hasn't psychology at least started that process by unifying the conscious and the unconscious?

Libby: No. There *is* no such perfect all-encompassing universal theory in psychology yet, any more than there is in physics.

'Isa: So what have you guys been doing for a century since Freud? Just fooling around?

Libby: Gathering data.

We know a lot about the conscious level, though certainly not everything. In fact, we don't even know what consciousness *is*, really.

How little psychology knows

And we know a little bit about the unconscious, though it's probably only about as much as Columbus knew about America when he first landed on the beach.

And we know just a few of the ways the unconscious influences the conscious, but we don't really know *how* the unconscious does that.

How little science knows

Evan: There's also no theory in science that successfully unifies those two levels in the physical sciences.

How little philosophy knows

'Isa: And there's no theory in philosophy that successfully unifies those two realms, physics and psychology, matter and spirit. The Theory of Everything would have to do that too.

Evan: So what do you do, as a philosopher, 'Isa, when you have a question as big as that and answers as little as that? How do you start?

'Isa: As a philosopher, I ask: What *kind of thinking* could ever come up with the kind of answer we're looking for?

Evan: And what do you answer?

"Whole-brain thinking"

'Isa: It must be a kind of "whole-brain" thinking that synthesizes "right brain" and "left brain" thinking. Do psychologists still use those terms, Libby?

Libby: Actually, that's the old, over-simplified way of speaking of them, and not quite correct in contemporary cybernetics. The whole brain is working, and not just one hemisphere, in each of the two kinds of thinking. But go on anyway. It's still *sort of* true. There *is* a distinction between poetry and mathematics, or intuition and analysis, or qualitative and quantitative thinking.

'Isa: The point about a formula, then, is that any universal theory couldn't be summarized in a formula because it would have to connect and synthesize the objects of two opposite kinds of thinking: what can be thought only by intuition, and thus transcends formulae, and also what can be thought by calculation, and is formulable. The theory itself can't be either of the two things it synthesizes. It has to synthesize synthesis and analysis.

Evan: And it would also have to *analyze* synthesis and analysis.

Libby: You mean it would have to be both holistic and discriminating.

Evan: Yes. In cybernetic terms, it has to be both analog and digital. Like the brain itself.

'Isa: Isn't it too materialistic to focus on the *brain?*

Evan: No, because all our physical instruments of knowing are filtered through the brain, both the instruments within our bodies – I mean our five senses – and the instruments outside our bodies – things like telescopes, computers, and libraries.

Subject and object also need to be unified.

Libby: But there's *another* division that has to be unified, because thinking not only has those two *powers* – intuition and calculation – but it also has two *poles*: the subject and the object, the thinker and the things thought about. That's why we need psychologists as well as physicists.

'Isa: You're right, Libby. Most of the scientists who theorize about a "theory of everything" are looking for a theory, and an "everything," that lies only on the object side, a theory of everything-that-can-be-thought-*about*. But a theory about everything-on-the-object-side has to be *thought* and *known* and *understood* on the *subject* side. So that side has to be included too somehow if the theory is going to be a Theory of Everything. Because subjectivity is part of Everything. It's real too.

Evan: But how could the subject be

known as an object of knowledge? How could it become part of the object without ceasing to be itself, without ceasing to be a subject?

How can the subject be known as an object?

'Isa: That's a classic philosophical problem.

Evan: And are there any philosophers who answer it?

'Isa: Existentialists and phenomenologists. They try to, anyway.

Evan: And what's the standard answer among those philosophers?

'Isa: That it *can't* be answered. Gabriel Marcel, for instance, says that the reason why philosophy has never solved problems like the union of mind and body, and the problem of evil, and understanding love, is because those problems are all part of the one unsolvable problem that Socrates set us back at the beginning, the problem of "know thyself." Marcel calls them "mysteries" rather than "problems" because they can't be objectified. We participate in the problem. We *are* part of the problem. He says, "a mystery is a problem which encroaches on its own data."

Problems vs. mysteries

Evan: Max Planck said something like Marcel said too, about physics. He said, "Science cannot solve the ultimate mystery of nature. And it is because, in the last analysis we ourselves are part of the mystery we are trying to solve."

Heisenberg's Indeterminacy Principle

That fits in nicely with the Copenhagen interpretation of the Heisenberg Indeterminacy Principle, or Uncertainty Principle. Are you familiar with that?

'Isa: Only vaguely. Can you give us a quick review?

Evan: According to Heisenberg, our act of observing either the position or the momentum of a subatomic particle changes the thing we're observing, so we can never observe both at the same time, we can never correlate these two things objectively and simultaneously.

'Isa: Why is it called the Indeterminacy Principle?

Evan: Because it states that either the position or the momentum is undetermined or uncertain in itself and open to change and determination from our very act of observing it.

'Isa: So if Marcel and Heisenberg are right, we will never find a Theory of Everything.

Evan: Do you agree with that, 'Isa?

'Isa: I don't know. Let's think about that for a minute – that's what philosophers do, you know: they don't just spout the first thing that comes into their head. Maybe we can still get a *partial* Theory of Everything.

Libby: That's a nice oxymoron!

'Isa: A Theory of Almost Everything, then. Let's suppose that the thinking subject can *not* be included in any objective theory. Let's suppose that the subject has to stay on the subject side while the object stays on the object side. Even then, even if the "Theory of Everything" is *only* a theory of every-thing-*on-the-object-side*, it's still a theory of *everything*-on-the-object-side. That's still something worthwhile that's never yet been found.

A Theory of *Almost* Everything?

And I think it follows from that that if it's going to be a theory of *everything*-on-the-object-side, it has to be thought or known or understood by *everything*-on-the-subject-side. And that means that it has to use both powers, both hemispheres, both inner eyes, so to speak. And that means a *psychological* "Theory of Everything," which is another worthwhile thing that hasn't been found yet.

Otherwise, if we don't use both eyes, then even if the theory were *true*, it would be *flat*. It would be like the world seen with only one eye: it would lack perspective; it would lack a whole dimension.

The depth dimension

Evan: I think I follow that. In the case of the physical eyes, that would be the third dimension of depth. And in the case of the mind's eye – the analytic mind's eye, anyway – it would be the fifth dimension.

'Isa: What do you mean by the fifth dimension?

Evan: The systemic unity of all four-dimensional events.

'Isa: Do I have to understand what that means to understand your theory?

Evan: Not really.

'Isa. Good. Go on, then.

Evan: It's traditionally believed that the typically Western mind, and the typically masculine mind . . .

Libby: Oh, oh. Here we go.

'Isa: Where are we going, Libby?

Sexist stereotypes?

Libby: Into the la-la land of sexist stereotypes.

'Isa: Shouldn't you wait to hear what Evan actually says before you label it? Maybe he's going to *demolish* the stereotypes.

Libby: Sure, like the Pope is going to demolish the Vatican. OK, sorry Evan, I'll shut up and let you finish.

Evan: As I said before I was so rudely interrupted – by both of you – the traditional view is that the Western mind and the masculine mind specializes in analytical thinking while the Eastern mind and the feminine mind specializes in intuitive thinking. I know it's a terribly oversimplified stereotype, but I think there's *something* to it. I can't believe it's just an accident that science arose in the West and mysticism in the East instead of vice versa; or that men instinctively tend to analyze things and distinguish them and define them, while women instinctively see connections and relationships. Or that men make war. For men, even love is like war. After all, his sexual organ is like a javelin, or a sword – something that splits space – while a woman's is like a spiderweb, or a house: something that unites.

Libby: I've heard this stuff before, you know – for, like, 2,000 years. All you're doing is turning up the stereo on the stereotype.

'Isa: It's not a stereotype; it's an archetype. Stereotypes are artificial.

Sexist archetypes?

Evan: Hear me out, Libby. My conclusion from this "stereotype" is that the Theory of Everything must be a joint effort of women as well as men, East as well as West, and poets and mystics as well as scientists and mathematicians.

'Isa: And the only discipline that does that is philosophy.

Libby: So we each need each other. Like the three legs of a tripod.

'Isa: What a typically feminine thing to say!

Libby: See? I told you. He's putting me down with his stereotypes.

'Isa: No, Libby, I'm putting you *up*. It's you who are putting yourself down. Think about it!

Conversation 2: Brain and Mind

'Isa: So Evan, do you think scientists need the help of philosophers to come up with their Theory of Everything?

Evan: Yes, I do. And also poets and musicians and mystics and maybe even surfers.

'Isa: What do you think philosophers can do?

Evan: Well, I certainly don't think any philosopher can come up with the Theory of Everything all by himself, but I think we scientists need you philosophers, maybe even as much as you need us.

'Isa: What is it that you think we philosophers can do for you?

Evan: What do *you* think you can do?

'Isa: Well, until a little less than a century ago, we thought we could get you into your castle. For two centuries, from

Philosophers' contribution to a Theory of Everything

Descartes through Hegel, throughout the so-called "Enlightenment," most philosophers created all-embracing metaphysical systems. They thought they could provide a more universal, overarching theory than any science could; a worldview or "big picture" that would integrate the sciences; a mental Map of Everything, although it wouldn't be a *scientific* Theory of Everything. But most philosophers don't think that any more.

No more "world-views"?

Evan: Didn't ancient and medieval philosophers think they could do that too, long before Descartes?

'Isa: In a less scientific sense, yes.

Evan: Why do you say "in a less scientific sense"?

'Isa: Because only since Descartes have philosophers distinguished philosophy and science and tried to imitate the scientific method in their philosophies.

Evan: But traditional philosophers set out metaphysical world views too, didn't they?

Aristotle, our Confucius

'Isa: Yes. For instance, Aristotle gave us a metaphysics and a cosmology and an epistemology and an anthropology and an ethics and a politics – a universal system, a way of thinking about everything, and it was probably the most successful and commonsensical set of categories in the history of Western civilization. We all think in Aristotelian categories. And Confucius did something like that for Chinese civilization.

Evan: And philosophers don't do that any more?

'Isa: No. After Hegel, just about all philosophers – at least the vast majority of English-speaking philosophers – backed off from building metaphysical systems. Most of them decided that philosophy should accept smaller, humbler tasks like clarifying language and logic instead. Instead of being the masters, they saw themselves as the servants, especially servants of scientists.

Evan: So philosophy is less influential than it used to be.

'Isa: And science is much *more* influential. And now the scientists, and you yourself, are hot on the trail of the biggest of "big pictures," a Theory of Everything. So do you see science as the leader of the expedition and philosophers as the servants, the porters?

Evan: No, 'Isa, I don't. Don't you remember what I said before? If it's the

Theory *of* Everything, it has to be known *by* everything, by a synthesis of every way of knowing. And that includes philosophy as well as science. It even includes poetry if poetry is a way of knowing.

Libby: Poetry too?

Evan: Poetry too.

Libby: I think that's a remarkable remark for you to make, Evan.

Evan: Why do you say that, Libby?

Libby: Because you have about as much poetry in your soul as that computer has.

The need for poetry, science, *and* philosophy

Evan: And you have about as much science in your soul as last night's dream has. See? That's why we need each other.

'Isa: And you both need a philosopher to mediate between you and to refute your two oversimplifications.

Evan: And that's not all. We also need good philosophers to refute bad philosophers.

'Isa: What bad philosophers?

Confusing mind and brain is bad philosophy.

Evan: The ones who confuse the mind with the brain. Some of them are called scientists, but they're really philosophers, because the question about the mind is a philosophical question, not a scientific question.

'Isa: I agree with you. But why do you need that refutation in particular?

Evan: Because the reduction of mind to brain clamps down on our big picture and makes it too small. It also clamps down on the instrument of seeing, and we'll never see the biggest picture with anything less than the biggest instrument.

'Isa: OK, I think I can refute that reductionistic philosophy for you in one sentence, Evan. Do you want it now?

Refuting reductionism

Evan: Please!

'Isa: Scientists study brains – in anatomy and physiology and cybernetics and brain chemistry – but psychologists study minds. Their fields overlap but they don't coincide. They're two different sciences. So from the sciences themselves comes the refutation of the reduction of one science to another, of psychology to physics.

1. Psychology is not just cybernetics

Evan: But suppose psychology is a pseudo-science? That's what the Marxist materialists say. Can you refute them?

'Isa: Easily. It's been done many times before. I'll give you two arguments: one from death and one from language.

Evan: And what, exactly, will they prove?

'Isa: That mind and brain are not the same.

Evan: If they're not the same, how do you say they're related?

'Isa: The brain is the physical instrument for thinking.

Evan: Not the source of thinking?

'Isa: No.

Evan: OK, prove it.

'Isa: That's easy.

Evan: And argue from facts, please.

2.
Death
removes no
molecules

'Isa: Is death enough of a fact for you?

Evan: If it isn't, I'm going to be very surprised some day.

'Isa: Then my first proof will be from the fact of death.

When you die, your brain is still physically present and intact, right?

Evan: It's *not* intact. It's not working any more.

'Isa: But no molecules disappear. It's *structurally* intact, it's just not functioning. The weight of a dead body one second after death is not one tiny bit less than one second before death. Experiments have proved this, with deathbeds placed on extremely sensitive scales.

Evan: All right, so what?

'Isa: Yet when we die the brain can't function, can't work any more.

Evan: Right.

'Isa: So *something* has disappeared, something that activated and enlivened this body and its brain.

Evan: The CPU went down, the Central Processing Unit.

'Isa: Most people call that the 'soul.'

Evan: But most scientists say they don't believe in the soul. And those that don't, don't because they can't find it anywhere, they can't bring it up on their computer screens.

Souls are like computer users.

'Isa: And that's like concluding that there's no person sitting at the keyboard of a computer because that person never appears on the screen. He couldn't, because he's not part of the information *or* part of the hardware *or* part of the software.

Evan: But I could put a picture of myself on the screen.

'Isa: Yes, but you couldn't put yourself there, only a picture.

Evan: I couldn't put a tree there either, only a picture of it.

'Isa: There's a difference. The only

3.
The irre-
ducibility of
subjectivity
to an object

reason you can't put a tree there is the lack of physical space. The reason you can't put yourself there is that you're a subject, not an object. Pictures are only objects. They can't think.

Evan: But I can think about you as an object. Yet you're a subject. So I can think about a subject as my object.

'Isa: Yes, and I can do the same to you, but I can't imagine a *picture* of my subjectivity, or of yours. I can conceive having my mind, or my consciousness, or my personality, or my soul, put into your body – I can write a science fiction story about that. And I can imagine our bodies, I can have a picture our two bodies. But I can't imagine a *picture* of our souls.

Evan: So what does that prove?

'Isa: That the soul is more than the body. And the mind is one of the powers of the soul, while the brain is one of the organs of the body. So that shows that the mind is more than the brain.

'Soul' =
'subject'

Evan: What, exactly, do *you* mean by the 'soul,' 'Isa?

'Isa: The soul is the unimaginable subject that's doing the act of imagining and thinking. It can be thought about, though, even though it can't be imagined, so it's both subject and object of thought. You can have a concept of the soul, but not an image. The soul does the imagining, but it can't be imagined. It has no size or color or shape.

Evan: What is the body then?

'Isa: The body, and especially the brain, is the soul's *instrument* for knowing. But it's not an external instrument like a telescope. It has eyes as the instruments for seeing, a nervous system as the instrument for feeling, and the brain, which is also part of the body, as the instrument for thinking.

Libby: That's not a proof, that's just an explanation.

'Isa: Call it what you will, there it is. If you follow it, it brings you beyond materialism.

Libby: I'm not a materialist – materialsts make lousy poets – but I'm not totally convinced by that, 'Isa. Do you have another argument?

'Isa: Yes. It's from language. The language we all use reveals this immaterial soul in the simplest of all words, the skinniest of all words, the word "I."

4. The meaningfulness of the word "I"

Libby: How do you know that that "I" is not just your brain?

'Isa: Because I call it "my" brain, as I call my body "my" body, which is saying that I am not it but its owner, its master, its user.

Libby: Maybe it's really your owner, master, and user. Maybe your brain pushes you around.

'Isa: Even then, I am not the same as it.

Libby: Are you saying your body is a mere object, like a house, and in that house there's another object, the brain, which is like a computer?

Body ≠ an object

'Isa: No. My body is me too. I can't take my body off, as I can take my clothes off. My body isn't "this old house." It's me too, because when you kill my body, you kill me, even though you don't kill my soul. I don't just *have* my body; I *am* my body.

And yet I also *have* my body, so that I can speak of using it, controlling it, or being controlled by it. And I can speak of losing it at death and still existing.

Libby: But maybe that's not *true*. You haven't *proved* life after death.

5.
The conceivability of life after death

'Isa: No, but whether there is life after death or not, it's meaningful: I can conceive it. And that means that the soul isn't simply the same as the body, because I have to conceive it differently. It has a different essence, a different nature, a different definition. It thinks. It doesn't take up space. It doesn't weigh anything. It isn't made of molecules. Including brain molecules.

Evan: What about the arguments the materialists use that claim that they can point to a material event for every so-called mental or spiritual event you can name, including abstract reasoning, moral choice, and even mystical experience? They can tell you what's going on in the brain physically every single time.

The scientific argument for materialism

'Isa: So what? What is that supposed to prove?

Evan: If you apply Ockham's Razor, it's supposed to prove that the soul is an unnecessary hypothesis. Because Ockham's Razor tells you always to choose the simplest hypothesis that explains all the data.

Ockham's Razor shaved down

'Isa: But Ockham's Razor is a reasonable principle only in science, not in philosophy. And it's only a practical principle, not a theoretical principle. It can't be used to prove anything.

Libby: What do you mean?

'Isa: It tells you not to think about

souls when you do brain chemistry – and that's good advice, but that doesn't mean there *are* no souls. Let's say you're a surgeon operating on your own mother. Ockham's Razor tells you to think of that body on the operating table simply as a machine that's not functioning perfectly, not as your mother, because that will make you a more efficient surgeon. And that's good practical advice, but that doesn't mean it *isn't* your mother.

The Razor also tells you not to think about God when you explain history, and that makes history more scientific, but that doesn't mean there *is* no God and no divine providence in history. If it does, then the Razor is just a camouflaged form of atheism. And as an assumption, not a conclusion. It's purely a priori.

6.
The direct experience of consciousness

And here's a second problem: using the Razor to reduce mind to brain *doesn't* explain all the data, because we experience consciousness as well as material objects of consciousness like molecular events in the brain that we can see.

And here's a third problem: if you do use the Razor, you can use it with just as much justification to cut away matter as to cut away mind. If every mental event can be explained by a material event, every material event can also be explained by a mental event, so Ockham's Razor can end up proving that matter is only a dream, or a projection of consciousness. As in some forms of Hinduism and Buddhism. And every material event *can* be explained as a mental event, because as soon as you *think* about a material event – any possible material event – that becomes a mental event because you're thinking about it.

7. Ockham's Razor can "prove" immaterialism too.

Thousands of philosophers have written thousands of articles with thousands of arguments in them about this question, the relation between mind and brain. I haven't refuted all the materialists' arguments with these few simple little points. But I hope it's enough to answer your question so that we can get on with Evan's Theory of Everything.

Libby: It's not enough for me.

Evan: But it's enough for me.

'Isa: And *that's* enough for me.

Conversation 3: Logic and Intuition

Libby: Why did we have to go through all that philosophical stuff about mind and brain? I thought we were just talking about Evan's Theory of Everything.

'First eye,' 'second eye,' and 'third eye'

Evan: Because the only instrument adequate for discovering the Theory of Everything is the 'third eye,' and there *is* no 'third eye' if materialism is true; there's only the 'first eye,' the ones made of molecules, the ones behind my glasses.

Libby: What's the 'second eye' then?

Evan: The rational mind. Even that doesn't exist according to materialism. There's just the brain, like a computer without a user and without a programmer.

To get to a Theory of Everything I think we have to go beyond even the 'second eye,' which is the rational mind, and talk about a 'third eye.'

Libby: That's the intuitive mind, right?

Evan: It's one of the powers of the intuitive mind.

Libby: Isn't intuition unscientific? Isn't science limited to 'first eye' and 'second eye' thinking? A combination of empiricism and rationalism?

Is intuition unscientific?

Evan: I don't think so. Even Einstein, you know, said that "the intuitive mind is a sacred gift and the rational mind is a faithful servant. We have created a society that honors the servant and has forgotten the gift."

And if it *is* unscientific, then I guess the Theory of Everything has to go beyond science to integrate science with Everything Else.

Libby: So the material brain is related only to the material eyes, the 'first eye'? Is that it?

Evan: No. All three 'eyes' use the brain. The optic nerve of the 'first eye' is physically connected to the brain. And the rational thinking done by the conscious mind is done with the brain, mainly by its cerebral cortex – that's what they used to think was done by the left hemisphere. And the intuitive thinking that's done by the deeper mind, including 'third

All three 'eyes' use the brain

{35}

eye thinking' – that uses the brain too – that's what they used to think was done by its right hemisphere.

Libby: So the 'third eye' is simply intuition?

Evan: No, it's not quite that simple ...

Libby: Why not?

The 'third eye' is only one of numerous powers of intuition

Evan: Because not all intuitive think-ing" is 'third eye' thinking. Everyone can intuit, but not everyone can open the 'third eye.'

Libby: Oh. I see.

1. ordinary feelings

'Isa: So you'd classify ordinary feel-ings as intuition too, then?

Evan: Yes.

'Isa: So there are at least two differ-ent kinds of intuition.

Evan: At least two. Probably more.

2. purely subjective feelings

'Isa: Let's see how many more, so that we don't confuse 'third eye thinking' with any other form of thinking. What about feelings? Aren't there purely subjec-tive feelings? For instance, depression, or joy, or pain, or pleasure, or vague fear with-out a specific object, or a kind of general-ized boredom, or the feeling of excitement and anticipation when you don't know exactly what you are anticipating?

Evan: Yes.

'Isa: And there are also object-oriented feelings, aren't there? Feelings *about* something – something other than the feeling subject himself? For instance, when you "just know" that a certain person is not trustable, or that a certain act is wrong?

3. feelings with objects

Evan: Yes, that too. So that's three forms of intuition so far.

'Isa: What about intellectual intuition? I mean the simple apprehension or understanding of a concept or a meaning without judging anything about it? For instance, simply understanding the meaning of "apple," or "man." That's *intellectual*, but not *rational*. It's intuition, but not feeling. It's intellectual intuition.

4. intellectual intuition

Evan: That too. So that's four.

'Isa: What about mystical intuition? Or is that the same as 'third eye thinking'?

5. mystical conscious-ness

Evan: I don't think it is the same.

'Isa: How would you define mystical intuition?

Evan: As a radically transformed consciousness that transcends the dualism or distinction between the subject-of-consciousness and the object-of-consciousness.

'Isa: And why isn't that the same as "third-eye thinking"?

'Third eye'
not mystical

Evan: Because mystical consciousness is very rare in all cultures, but 'third eye thinking' is rare only in modern Western culture.

'Isa: That's true. So mysticism is a *fifth* form of intuition?

Evan: Yes.

Libby: I think this "third-eye thinking" is *un*conscious, while your other forms of intuition are all conscious. But there are a lot more things the unconscious does besides "third-eye thinking." Should we try to list them too?

Evan: That would be too long, and too controversial, I think.

Uncon-
scious
depths in
myths and
fairy tales

Libby: Maybe we should look at some of the old stories of "third-eye thinking" from ancient cultures. Because it seems to be buried deep in the memory of human culture, just as it's buried deep in the unconscious. And maybe that's why most forms of it seem to us moderns to be nothing but myths or fairy tales.

Evan: But don't the myths and fairy tales seem sometimes like gleams of something beautiful and profound emerging like bubbles of light from dark swamps of childish nonsense?

'Isa: I don't see any bubbles. I just see the nonsense.

Libby: That's because you're ignorant of psychology.

Evan: Well, *I* see some bubbles. And I want to harness the bubbles.

'Isa: But even if they're there, how do you do that?

Evan: I don't know.

'Isa: We need an instrument.

Evan: We don't have one.

'Isa: Then we need to make one. We need to make a harness, a bubble-harnessing instrument.

Evan: How do we do *that*? What instrument do we use to make that harnessing instrument?

'Isa: Maybe we already have it in the 'third eye.'

Libby: All that 'third eye' stuff sounds interesting to a psychologist like me, but it must sound terribly unscientific to a scientist like you, Evan. There's no science of the 'third eye,' is there?

No science of the 'third eye'

Evan: Not yet.

Libby: And maybe never.

Evan: Maybe never.

Libby: So it might always remain a mystery to science.

No scientist is only a scientist.

Evan: Maybe. But a scientist is always more than a scientist.

Libby: What do you mean?

Evan: I mean only a human being can be a scientist. And a scientist is a human being before he is a scientist. A whole human being. I am Evan the human before I am Evan the scientist.

'Isa: But how do you open the 'third eye'? There must be a way, if that eye exists, and if some people have actually done it.

Libby: We need another whole dialog for that. I think I know a little more about that than you do.

'Isa: Why? Because you're a woman?

Libby: Maybe. And also because I'm a surfer.

'Isa: You didn't mention the fact that you were a psychologist.

Libby: First things first.

Conversation 4:
How to Open the 'Third Eye'

'Isa:　Logically, if we need 'third eye-thinking' for the Theory of Everything, we need some way of opening the 'third eye.'

Libby:　Maybe we don't.

'Isa:　Of course we do. Because most of us don't do 'third-eye thinking,' and don't know how. And our culture doesn't do it, and can't show us how. Only a few unusual individuals do it. We need some way to change that if we're going to get to the Theory of Everything.

Why we need a method for opening the 'third eye'

Libby:　Maybe we don't.

'Isa:　You mean maybe we can get to the Theory of Everything without 'third-eye thinking'?

Why we don't

Libby:　No.

'Isa:　Are you saying, then, that we should look for a mystic to do it for us? Under "M" in the Yellow Pages, maybe?

Libby: No.

'Isa: Are you saying we should just give up? Because that's the only logical alternative left.

Libby: How logical we are today! Did you ever consider the possibility that that's precisely your problem?

'Isa: Frankly, no. I never thought being logical was a problem, or that being illogical was a solution.

Libby: Well, there's a logic to thinking that it *is* your problem.

'Isa: Libby, did you ever hear of the law of non-contradiction?

Libby: Jack, did you ever hear the word "paradox"? [Editor's Note: "Jack" is 'Isa's nickname. He feels ambivalent about it because Muslims aren't supposed to have nicknames – which is why Libby uses it when she wants to get under his skin.]

Evan: I think there *is* a logic to what Libby says. It's a well-known psychological phenomenon, and there are many everyday examples of it, aren't there, Libby?

The 'third eye' sees when we stop other thinking.

Libby: Sure. Freudian slips, for instance. They come out only when the part of your mind that does logic and analysis and definition and control sleeps a little.

Seeing a faint object is another example. If you stare directly at a faint star in the sky, you won't see it, but if you stop staring and relax and look a little to the side, you can see it.

Examples of this principle

Sports are full of examples. Just the other day, I won at bowling because I confused the anchorman on the other team by calling his attention to his perfect form. I said, "You have the best form I've ever seen, and I've read a lot of books on how to bowl but none of them tell me what to do with your right hand when you bowl if you're a left-handed bowler. What do *you* do?" He said he didn't know, he had never thought about it. So I told him I'd be watching him. You can guess what happened. He bowled thirty pins under his average.

Still another example is dozens of the arts in the East: for instance archery in Zen Buddhism. You don't shoot the arrow, you let it shoot itself. Or in Chinese landscape painting, you don't paint the landscape, you just let it paint itself.

So I think the way to 'third-eye thinking' isn't *doing* anything at all, but just *stopping* something, stopping the other kind of thinking: rational thinking, controlled thinking.

'Isa: Frankly, I'm a little suspicious of that. Losing control – that sounds like losing responsibility. That's fine for pantheists, maybe, but not for me.

"Surrender" Libby: But that's the whole point of religion, isn't it? To surrender yourself to God? Isn't that the very essence of Islam, 'Isa?

'Isa: Yes, it is. But that's different.

Libby: The object is different, yes: there's no God in Buddhism, for instance. But the subjective state isn't different. You get out of the way.

"Faith" Evan: She's right, 'Isa. In both Christianity and Islam, you don't try to save yourself, or eternalize yourself, or reward yourself. You let God do it. It's called faith, trust. That's a kind of letting-go. And you also have to repent, which means letting go of your sins, your evil.

Libby: It's like dissolving the bad glue that glues you to your sins before you can get the good glue, the God glue that glues you to God. You understand that, don't you, 'Isa?

'Isa: Of course. But religious faith is

for everybody. It's not an example of 'third-eye thinking.'

Libby: We're not saying it is. We're just making a psychological analogy.

'Isa: OK. I see the common psychological point: the letting-go.

Libby: There are some scientific analogies in cognitive psychology too, especially in cybernetics.

Evan: What did they find there?

Libby: They were looking for some correlation between brain activity and paranormal states of consciousness like ESP and telepathy and mystical experiences or deep meditation. This was the Newberg and D'Aquili study, I think. They expected to find some area of the brain that was more active, or "lit up," during those states of consciousness, but instead they found that certain areas of the brain became *less* active, or "dark."

The brain correlate to ESP

Evan: What part of the brain was it?

Libby: It was in the posterior superior parietal lobe.

Evan: What does that do?

Libby: It distinguishes you from the rest of the world. It orients you. It tells you you're separate from everything else, that you're in your body instead of out of it.

'Isa: Well, that makes sense. Those famous "out-of-body experiences" are just tricks of the brain.

How to see things 1,000 miles away

Libby: No, they're not, because in these experiences you get all sorts of real powers clicking in, like seeing things a thousand miles away, and reading other minds. And there are just too many well-documented cases of that happening to dismiss them all as hoaxes or hallucinations – unless you're a fundamentalist materialist and your dogma requires it.

The point is that once you get yourself out of the way, all sorts of things can start happening, even things like seeing stuff a thousand miles away, because we're all connected to everyone and everything else in the universe, in ways that ordinary consciousness suppresses.

'Isa: I'm skeptical, Libby. That sounds like pantheism to me.

Libby: No it isn't. It doesn't mean that everything is one, or everything is God. It just means everything is connected.

Because everything is connected

Evan: And that's exactly what science is discovering: that everything is connected, in more ways, and more subtle ways, and more complex ways, than we ever thought.

'Isa: But how do you know that the powers that are released in this state of consciousness aren't demonic powers that are deceiving you?

Libby: The point isn't the powers. They're just by-products. The point is the state of consciousness itself, or rather what it reveals about the universe: how connected we are with it. And that's what people who have these powers almost always say: that the powers are less important than everybody thinks, that it isn't the powers but the philosophy, the wisdom that it brings, that's valuable.

Paranormal consciousness more important than paranormal powers

And that's valuable to us because it gives us a kind of Unified Field Theory of mind.

'Isa: Have you ever experienced any of these "paranormal powers"?

Libby: Yes.

'Isa: More than once?

Libby: Almost every time I surf. I can actually feel or sense a wave coming before I ever see it. I'll be just sitting on my board, and nothing has happened for ten minutes, and suddenly I get this feeling that I need to paddle *there* instead of *here*, and it works. There it is. The wave comes. We're just connected, me and the wave.

Surfing as paranormal consciousness

'Isa: But you said a few minutes ago that we could never find a method of turning on the 'third eye.'

Libby: Not by looking for it. But it can come, like the dawn. We just have to stop being stupid roosters who think our crowing brings up the sun. We have to shut up.

Evan: As Job did. And only then did God show up.

Work on the eyelid, not the eye

Libby: You see, the 'third eye' *is* already "turned on." But there's an eyelid closing it. All we have to do – all we *can* do – is move the eyelid, get the eyelid out of the way. We don't work on the eye but on the eyelid. There's no method for turning on the 'third eye,' only for turning off the other two. It's like turning off the ceiling light so you can see the faint glow inside the night-light. Or like waiting for the evening to turn off the sun so you can see the stars.

If you try to turn it on, if you try to *find* your 'third eye' as an object you can define or a power you can use, you just won't be able to do it. And that's because the kind of consciousness we use when we *try* to do anything is logical and practical consciousness. It's logical because we need a definite concept of what we want to do, and it's practical because we have a definite desire to do it. Those are the two parts of the eyelid that have to move, have to get out of the way, for the 'third eye' to work: concepts and desires. So, you see, the more you try to *make* it work, the less it can work.

That's why whenever scientists experiment with ESP or clairvoyance or anything like that, the results are much less clear than they want: because it can't be deliberately replicated. They find a person with these special mental gifts, and they see the person producing spectacular results, and they try to repeat them, and the results just don't come the second time. That happens over and over again.

Why experiments with ESP fail

It's like what Freud said about accessing the unconscious: you have to let your attention float free; you have to let go.

'Isa: You know, even old Aristotle said something like that. He said that if you want to write poetry, you should lie down on your back, but if you want to solve intellectual problems, you should walk around. His disciples were called the "peripatetics," which means the "walkers-around," because that's how they philosophized.

Aristotle's version of the same principle

What Aristotle advised for poets sounds like what Freud advised for patients who want to discover their unconscious: lie down on your back as if you're floating.

Libby: Exactly.

'Isa: But when you lie down, you tend to go to sleep. How do you stay active?

Surfing your unconscious

Libby: By *surfing* your unconscious. You're carried on thought waves, just as I'm carried on water waves. But you're *more* alert and active the more the wave takes over. No surfer ever went to sleep on a wave. That's why I think surfing is the perfect way to access that state of mind. But it's got to be soul-surfing, not hot-dogging.

Evan: If Einstein had only been a surfer. . . .

Conversation 5: Matter and Spirit

Evan: Here's one very simple way of approaching what 'Isa asked for: a way of doing 'third-eye thinking.' Have you ever noticed how little we *notice*, out of all that we *see*? And how little we see, out of all that is to be seen? And how little there is to be seen, out of all there is?

Being > Seeing > Noticing

Libby: How do you know there's more than what you see? You're a scientist.

Evan: It's precisely *because* I'm a scientist that I say that.

Libby: But a scientist has to go by what he sees.

Evan: And that's how I know there's more than what I see: what I see tells me that.

How we know there is more than we see

Libby: Are you saying that modern science is coming back to the ancient world view, with spirits and magic and all that?

Evan: No, but something like it. Something more than the Big Machine.

'Isa: Something more than matter, at least.

Matter as "the outside of reality"

Evan: Yes. The ancient world view, in all cultures, claims that the matter we see is only the outside of reality, so to speak, the manifestation of something more, something that's not just more *matter* but something that's more *than* matter – more than what we ordinarily mean by matter, anyway. So according to this world view, matter is like the scrim of a stage set.

'Isa: Like the epidermis of a body.

Libby: Like the surf.

Evan: What do you mean, like the surf?

Libby: The surface. The surf-face. The face of the surf. The sea is more than the surf.

Evan: Something like that, yes.

Libby: So when we see something, that's only the waves of the great sea of being crashing against the shore of our consciousness.

Matter looks immaterial.

Evan: Something like that, yes. The more science explores matter, the more immaterial it looks. It's certainly not simple. And it's not solid. It's like the surface of a sea, and we haven't gotten to the bottom of it yet. It may be bottomless. We're always discovering more levels of depth after we think we've penetrated to the bottom. And everything comes out of this sea, like babies from a womb.

Libby: That's why the ancients called it "Mother Earth."

Evan: Yes. They were right. It's full, not empty. What we usually call emptiness, or "empty space," or "outer space," is only the absence of *matter* – actually, it's not quite even a complete absence of matter; it's *almost* a vacuum, but not quite. The ancients never called it "space." They called it "the heavens." To them it was full, not empty. It was like a womb.

Space is not empty.

Libby: What's it full of?

'Isa: Potentiality.

Evan: That's   what   philosophers would call it. Scientists would call it Energy. An energy that produces matter, or manifests as matter. Matter seems to be something like the freezing or solidifying of energy.

'Isa: So it isn't correct to see energy simply as one of matter's properties?

Matter as frozen energy

Evan: Probably   not.   Matter   seems

more relative to energy than energy to matter.

Libby: It's something like the sea and the land, then.

Evan: What do you mean?

Libby: I mean the sea is like energy, or it's a symbol of energy, and the land is like matter. The sea is bigger than the land. The land is just an island in the sea rather than the sea being just a large lake inside the land.

Sea and land as symbols of energy and matter

Evan: That's a good image. Because the sea is full of energy. It's never still. It's always breathing waves.

'Isa: And the sea is also full of potentiality to take any shape, depending on the shape of the matter of the vessel it fills. That's why the ancients were so terrified of floods: it was a reversion to formlessness, to the primal chaos, before things took solid shape, before the Creator said, "Let there be *this* and *that*."

The sea as potentiality

Libby: So water suggests a kind of ontological insecurity. I guess that's one reason why surfing is so thrilling: it's like a time machine that takes you back before creation. That's why it's more thrilling than doing essentially the same thing on land: snowboarding or snow tubing or

Water as ontological insecurity

skiing or sand dune tobogganing. When you surf, you feel like you're surfing on *energy*, not matter.

Evan: But the two are convertible. Matter can be converted into energy and energy into matter. So deep down they must be the same thing. We just don't have a word for that one thing.

Libby: Matter converts into energy in nuclear fission, right?

Evan: Yes. Or nuclear fusion.

Libby: And when does energy convert into matter?

Evan: Throughout all of time. Everything that has ever happened in nature since the Big Bang has been energy becoming different forms of matter. Or matter destroying its old forms, dying, regressing into potential energy before it takes another actual material form. We don't notice that because it's usually as gradual as a nuclear explosion is sudden.

'Isa: What about *spiritual* energy? The energy of thinking and willing? That's a kind of energy too. And that converts into something like matter when it solidifies into specific thoughts and specific deeds. How is that spiritual energy

Everything = energy converting into matter

Spiritual energy too

{55}

related to the physical energy that converts into physical matter?

Evan: That's a deep philosophical question.

'Isa: And can you as a scientist give me as a philosopher any principles I can use to help solve it?

One university ∴ one energy

Evan: Yes, I think so. The most obvious one is that the universe is a *uni*-verse, a single continuum, more like a single enormous field of energy than an empty space. Everything touches everything, everything influences everything. So the different forms of energy can't be simply different and unrelated. We're not living in two universes, a spiritual universe and a material universe, but in only one universe. So those two different energies have to be at root one and the same. Because whenever we see something like this anywhere in the universe – two parallel forces that follow the same pattern – however different these two things are and however apparently irreducible to each other they are, they always turn out to be manifestations or effects or functions of some deeper, more fundamental, more universal, underlying unity.

'Isa: So physical energy and spiritual energy must be a single energy, like a single tree-trunk that branches into two main branches.

Evan: Something like that, yes. But our modern minds are like monkeys that live in the upper branches, while the ancient mind was like – like a fungus that lived in the trunk.

'Isa: That sounds pretty insulting to the ancient mind.

Libby: Not at all. It's good psychology. That's the psychosomatic unity, the mind and the body being not two things but two branches of the same tree, two dimensions of one and the same person. And we know that unity from inside, sort of like the fungus in the trunk. You call that unity your self. You know you are a self, or have a self. And you know that it's just one self – unless you're insane, unless you're a "split personality," or "possessed." Yet that single self – that *you* – is both invisible and visible. It's both psyche and soma. So I guess we are the key to the universe, then, huh?

The psychosomatic unity as the key to the cosmos

Evan: I think you are onto something big there, Libby. Yes. Because the place where we can discover this principle of the unity of the two energies most easily and most certainly is in ourselves. But that doesn't mean that the universe is a self, or thinks, as we do, or has a mind or a soul. It doesn't mean the universe is a single person. That's pantheism, I think.

Libby: But can't you say that the universe thinks in us? That it comes to a point in us? Can't you say that the universe "humans" as a flower "flowers"? That we are the brains of the universe? The instruments it uses to think with?

Evan: In a word, no, Libby. At least that's not what I'm saying. That *is* pantheism – either old Hindu mysticism or flaky New Age stuff.

The New Age Movement vs. the Old Age Movement

Libby: And what you were saying before *isn't* New Age stuff?

Evan: No.

Libby: It sounded like it to me.

Evan: No, it was the Old Age Movement, not the New Age Movement.

Libby: What's the difference?

Humanity: the key to the universe

Evan: The New Age Movement is pantheism. This isn't. It's something more like humanism. Because it sees the human "I" as the supreme key to the universe. New Age pantheism is the opposite, I think. It's like Buddhism: it sees the "I" as the supreme *illusion*, the great *obstacle* to enlightenment.

Libby: Oh. Why did they look so alike then, if they're so opposite?

Evan: Think of two ships leaving the same port. The port is familiar. It symbolizes ordinary consciousness. The two ships start there, at the dock, but they both leave that dock, that land, for the open sea. And that fact so impresses you that it seems to you that they're going to the same place. You don't see the land they're sailing toward. It's too far away. All you see is the sea. And it's the same sea, and it's not your familiar land. So since all you notice is the common negative – *not* the land – you think the two ships are going on an identical voyage, even though one may be going to Iceland and the other may be going to South Africa.

Not all mysticism is the same

Libby: So 'third-eye humanism' is like South Africa and pantheism is like Iceland?

Evan: Yes, that's the symbolism.

'Isa: So then, Evan, are you saying that these two cosmic energies, spiritual and material, are unified in us?

Evan: Yes.

'Isa: And one is mind and the other is matter?

Evan: Yes. Or more broadly, one is spiritual and the other is material.

'Isa: So they're like soul and body.

Evan: Yes.

'Isa: Then are they the soul and the body of the same "I"?

Body and soul directly proportional

Evan: In you, yes. That's why as you increase or decrease either one, you produce a corresponding increase or decrease in the other one. For instance, mental depression tends to cause physical exhaustion and physical exhaustion tends to cause mental depression. We hug and kiss each other because we're happy and we're happy because we hug and kiss each other. It's like the words and the meaning of a book, or the notes and the feelings of a piece of music: if you change either one, you change the other, and the only way to change either one is to change the other.

'Isa: If they're one in us, are they also one in the universe outside us?

Evan: That's the million-dollar question. I think they have to be united everywhere, somehow, although in a lesser way, a more diffuse way, than they are united in us. I think we are the "radium points" of the universe.

"Radium points"

Libby: What's a "radium point"?

{60}

Evan: I was explaining that to 'Isa before. When the Curies discovered radioactivity, they discovered it only in one element, radium. But they assumed that it couldn't possibly be an anomaly, a singularity, a kind of freak. They assumed that it had to be only the protuberance, so to speak, of something that was everywhere. Like an island. An island is only that part of the underground mountain chain that pokes up above the water where we can see it. There's always more underwater. So the Curies started looking for this new force in other elements, and they found it, and discovered one of the fundamental forces of the universe, radioactivity.

So I like to call any such protuberance a "radium point." Hitler, for instance.

Libby: Hitler?

Evan: Sure. He's human, isn't he? And therefore there's got to be a Hitler in ourselves too. That was the title of a book by a German philosopher with a French name, Max Picard, that he wrote right after World War II: "Hitler in Ourselves." Great title, eh?

'Isa: Scary title. Scary as Hell. Literally.

Hitler was a "radium point."

Evan: But when you see a saint, you have to say the same thing: There goes a "radium point." And so you have to look for the Mother Teresa in ourselves as well as the Hitler in ourselves.

'Isa: Do you Christians also say you can find the God in ourselves? Is that who you say Jesus is?

Evan: No, no. We believe God is just as transcendent as you Muslims do. We also believe something that you don't: that He became immanent, He became incarnate, He *became* a man, Jesus, by a supernatural miracle. But we don't believe that God is in us as our human nature is in us, or as the universe is in us, or as we are in the universe, or even as we are in each other.

Does the Theory of Everything include God?

'Isa: So how does God factor into this Theory of Everything, Evan?

Evan: God's not part of Everything, so the theory doesn't include God.

'Isa: Good. I was worried . . .

Libby: But God created and designed the universe, right? You both believe that, right? So all the design that we see in the universe, all that science sees too, has got to come from Him, right?

Evan: Right.

Libby: And we see that design, don't we?

Evan: If our 'third eye' is open, yes. We don't see design with the eyes in our head, or with our "left-brain" computer. Computers can't see holistic designs. Design isn't a mathematical concept. It's not a concept you can quantify. So you can't use it in an exact science. "Intelligent design" isn't a scientific theory.

How do we perceive design?

'Isa: What is it, then?

Evan: Any ancient culture would say it's common sense, because the 'third eye' was part of common sense to them. If it's not that to us, that's because we've closed our third eye. Or because we don't trust it.

"Intelligent design" not science

'Isa: So with this 'third eye' what do you say we can see? God? Or just God's design in the universe?

Evan: We don't see God. We see only a little of His design. Very little. Like the backside of the tapestry that He weaves. The tapestry is the universe and our lives in it.

Cosmos as a tapestry

'Isa: But that means that we can at least guess at the design on the other side of the tapestry from the clues we have on this side.

Evan: Yes.

'Natural the-
ology'?

'Isa: I don't know if I can buy that. As a Muslim, I'm suspicious of "natural theology." I believe God has to speak and reveal Himself to us if we're going to know anything about Him. That's why the Qur'an tells us so much more than natural reason does about God.

Evan: Of course it does. But that doesn't mean nature doesn't tell us anything at all about Him.

'Isa: What does it tell us? Guesses, that's all.

Evan: Maybe so. But guesses can be good guesses.

'Isa: What makes one guess better than another, then?

Analogies
to God?

Evan: Guesses are stimulated by analogies, so the best guess would be stimulated by the best analogy. And the best analogy is the richest, fullest analogy. And the richest analogy for *everything*, and therefore for the Creator of everything, is ourselves.

'Isa: We Muslims don't say that man was created in the image of God, as you Christians do. I think I have a theological problem with that.

Souls as
mirrors

Evan: But it doesn't depend on theology. It's philosophy. Didn't old

Aristotle say that "the soul is, in a way, all things"? Because it can know all things in the universe, as a mirror can reflect everything in a room?

'Isa: I'll suspend judgment on that if you don't mind. Let's get back to your Theory of Everything.

Evan: What do you want to know about it?

'Isa: Well, to start with, I want to know where you find data for it.

Conversation 6: The *Data*

Evan: That's a legitimate question, 'Isa. There's no science without data. All hypotheses are relative to data, tested by data.

'Isa: So where are the data for your Theory of Everything?

Evan: You're a logical person, 'Isa. You know the answer to that question.

'Isa: No, I don't.

Where do we look for data?

Evan. Sure you do. Tell me, where would a scientist find the data for a theory of light?

'Isa: I don't know. Where?

Evan: Of course you know. In light! And where would a scientist find the data for a theory of sleeping?

'Isa: In sleeping.

Evan: And where would a scientist find the data for a theory of tectonic plates?

'Isa: In tectonic plates.

Evan: So where would a scientist find the data for a Theory of Everything?

'Isa. In everything. I see. But there's a problem with that. There's a law of logic that fouls up your analogy there. It says that any concept loses comprehension as it gains extension, loses meaning and specificity as it gains generality. The less specific anything is, the harder it is to identify. Which means you have a big problem with that concept of 'everything.' It's too big. It's everything in general so it's nothing in particular. 'Everything' is hardly an identifiable database. To us, anyway. Only God has access to that broad a database. And you're not God.

Evan: Did you think I forgot that unfortunate little fact?

'Isa: Well, yes, frankly. Because sometimes that most obvious fact in the world is the hardest to remember. That's why we Muslims keep reminding ourselves of it at least five times a day: "There is no God but God." You can summarize the whole Qur'an in four words. God is telling us just two things: "I'm God" and "You're not." And it's that second thing that's the hardest for us to remember.

(margin note) 'Everything' has no specificity.

(margin note) Only two God-facts

Evan: I'll try to remember that.

'Isa: Seriously, you have a big problem at the very beginning of your journey of exploration down the river of discovery into the ocean of everything. You said that your data is everything, but since you're not God, you don't have access to that data. And since you admitted that a theory is relative to its data, that means you can't get your theory.

No access to 'Everything'?

Evan: But we have "radium points," remember. We have special areas of data that function as microcosms for the whole of the data, points where universal principles show themselves more clearly and specifically.

'Isa: But even there, you've only got "radium points" for areas much narrower than "everything" – for instance, chemistry, when you speak of the Curies, or human good and evil, when you speak of Hitler or Mother Teresa. Where will you find your "radium points" for *everything*?

Evan: My answer is going to sound flaky to you. And maybe it's the wrong answer. But before I give you my answer, I want to give you my principle. Because even if my answer is wrong, my principle isn't, and we can use it to find another answer.

'Isa: OK. What's your principle?

Evan: Analogy. I'm looking for an analogy to radium. Now the formula for an analogy is a proportion: A is to B as C is to D. So here, A is to everything as radium is to radioactivity, and as Hitler and Mother Teresa are to human good and evil, or as volcanoes are to the earth's molten core.

'Isa: All right, so what are your volcanoes for everything?

Evan: I think there are quite a few of them. I'd like to review some of the ones you find in most popular science books, and then I'd like to suggest one that the books seem to forget, the one that makes me think that just maybe Libby is the most important resource for our theory – and that's waves.

But before we look at waves, let's look at some other clues, some other "volcanoes." All these different volcanoes come from the same core of the earth, so even if we can't directly see the core, we can know something about it from intuiting the unity of all the volcanoes, so to speak, by tracing back the volcanoes to their unifying principle.

Analogies to radium

"Volcanoes" from Everything

'Isa: That sounds promising. Go ahead, give us some good "pop science," Evan.

Brain waves and radio waves

Evan: One piece of data comes from the coordination between the human brain and the universe. To put it very simply, our "brain waves" match the universe's waves, for instance radio waves, in too many ways to be mere coincidence. For instance, there's the Schuman Resonance. That's a natural radio wave, a standing wave that keeps resonating around the earth. It beats at exactly 7.8 Hz. And the dominant brain frequency of all vertebrate animals, including man, is also 7.8 Hz. There's one exception: people in modern Western industrial cultures. Their frequency is usually higher. But psychics, mystics, shamans, and healers register a 7.8 Hz brain wave.

Libby: Where does that Schuman Resonance thing come from? Could it come from the planet itself? Is the whole planet one big brain?

Evan: No. A wave doesn't necessarily mean a thought. But isn't it interesting that the frequency of the 'third eye' and the frequency of the planet are the same?

Here's another amazing fact. It's called

Bell's Theorem, and the Einstein-Podolsky-Rosen Paradox. Experiments have definitely proved this. Take two particles that have lived together, so to speak, for a long time as a two-particle system. Now separate them and send them into opposite ends of the world, or even opposite ends of the universe, with no physical connection between them any more. Now change the state of one of those particles, and instantly you'll see the exact equivalence of a change happening in the other particle, without any discernable or even theoretically knowable physical cause moving between the two particles.

Bell's Theorem

Libby: It sounds as if they're having mental telepathy with each other. That's spooky.

Evan: That's what Einstein called it: "spukhafte Fernwirkungen," "spooky action at a distance."

"Spooky action at a distance"

'Isa: Congratulations, Libby. Two great minds always think the same thoughts. Maybe your mind and Einstein's are those two particles.

Libby: This was actually proved by experiments? It's not just theory?

Evan: Yes. In 1982, by a guy named Aspect. Two identical photons were shot out of a calcium atom in opposite directions, and when one of them was altered, that alteration registered in the other one like a fingerprint.

Libby: How do scientists explain that?

Quantum particles like Catholic marriage

Evan: It's a principle of quantum mechanics. The two particles have to be treated as one indivisible whole, like a Catholic marriage. They can't really get divorced, ever.

'Isa: Is that true only for subatomic particles and Catholic marriages?

Koshima monkey telepathy?

Evan: Maybe not. The same phenomenon seems to have happened in Japan with the monkeys on Koshima Island, off the coast of southern Japan. In 1954 a little group of monkeys there started to eat potatoes in a new way, and four years later monkeys all over Japan had started doing the same thing even though there was no physical connection between the Koshima monkeys and the other monkeys, and there was no common cause in the environment that made both groups do that.

'Isa: Was that monkey telepathy, or what? How do scientists account for that, then?

Energy fields

Evan: Not by the ordinary rules of causality, but by a kind of field theory. In modern physics, fields are more basic than matter. Fields can't be explained in terms of matter, but matter has to be explained in terms of fields. And these fields are energy fields, and this seems to be true of all of the many different kinds of energy, including mental energy as well as physical energy.

A similar phenomenon is found in quarks. Unlike atoms, they can't be split. Or, rather, the hadron they're embodied in can't be split into any smaller parts. Quarks appear only in relationships of two or three, never alone.

Libby: That sounds like the Trinity!

'Isa: Let's stick to science, please. Tell me, Evan, can scientists correlate the physical energies they observe with brain activity, either in general or in particular?

Evan: What kind of correlation are you thinking of?

'Isa: I don't know. I just wonder whether the brain works in the same way as the universe works.

Evan: In some ways, the answer is yes. For instance, remember what we said earlier about why we were wrong to think of the "left brain" and the "right brain" as two parts that functioned semi-independently.

Brains function like holograms.

We now know that the whole brain functions like a hologram.

'Isa: What, exactly, is a hologram?

Evan: If you take a holographic photo of a cat and cut out one part of it, say its tail, and then enlarge just that section – the tail – to the size of the original photo, you will get not a big picture of the tail but a picture of the whole cat. Because the whole is contained in each of the parts.

The whole is not the sum of its parts.

'Isa: So that proves the old saying right: the whole is not just the sum of its parts.

Evan: Not in an organism, anyway. And that comes out in a hologram, in the same way as the DNA in any cell can tell you what you want to know about the whole animal, so you can clone the whole animal from just one cell.

So the brain functions as a hologram. It receives bioelectric frequencies and it interprets them not at any local part of the brain but throughout the whole brain.

Libby: Sort of like the CIA spying on the whole world but not just from the central office in Washington but from every blade of grass in the country?

Evan: Sort of.

'Isa: Isn't the information localized

in the brain, as it is in a computer's memory?

Evan: No. That's how the brain is *not* a computer. The information is spread throughout the whole brain and the whole nervous system too, along a very complex network of very fine fibers on all the nerve cells – and maybe even beyond them in some way in every cell in the body. So it's your whole body that thinks.

How brains are *not* computers

'Isa: How do we know that? What's the physical fingerprint of the information?

Evan: Waves. Frequency patterns. That's why even though I'm fascinated by all of these bits of data, these "radium volcanoes," as we called them, the one I'm most interested in is waves.

'Isa: What kind of waves?

Evan: All kinds of waves. Both physical and spiritual waves. Water waves and radio waves and gravity waves and brain waves and telepathy waves, if they exist . . .

Kinds of waves

Libby: And love waves too?

Evan: Yes, because they exist too. Science just hasn't looked at them yet.

Isa: If "love waves" include the cycles of a woman's period, science has looked at that, hasn't it?

Moon-and-menstru-ation coordination

Evan: But not deeply enough. For instance, science hasn't yet fully explained the coordination between them and the phases of the moon.

Libby: Wouldn't this have to apply to the psychological cycles of romance, as well as the physical cycles of menstruation?

Evan: Yes. That's data too.

'Isa: How can love be scientific?

Libby: Haven't you heard? It's love that makes the world go round.

Love = gravity

'Isa: But how can you put love and gravity together in the same formula?

Evan: Because the universe does. Because love is spiritual gravity. Because gravity is "love between particles." Love is a kind of gravity and gravity is a kind of love.

'Isa: I see the analogy. But . . . *romance?*

Evan: Did you ever hear *La Traviata*?

'Isa: The opera? Yes.

The pulse of the universe

Evan: Do you remember the line in Act I where Verdi says of romance that it is "the pulse of the universe"?

'Isa: That's just poetry, not science.

Evan: But how can a "science of everything" ignore anything, even poetry?

Tell me, 'Isa, did you ever read Dante's *Divine Comedy*?

'Isa: Yes.

Evan: Do you remember the last line? It comes at the mystical summit of all human knowledge, where Dante sees the mind of God, and sees the whole universe and all of human life in it from a God's-eye point of view. And what he says he sees is "the love that moves the sun and all the stars." That's the summit of our knowledge of the universe: the knowledge of cosmic, universal love.

'Isa: That's theology, not science.

Evan: But Dante thought theology was the highest science.

Libby: And that's the greatest line from the greatest poem from the greatest poet in the world.

Evan: And how can a science of everything ignore theology and poetry?

'Isa: But the universe of matter and the universe of spirit are two very different universes. They work by different laws, and they require different explanations, different *kinds* of explanation. For instance, matter is competitive but spirit isn't; anything material, like money, is divided and diminished when it's shared,

Dante as scientist

but things that are spiritual, like love and knowledge, multiply and increase when they're shared.

Matter and spirit not two universes

Evan: That's true, but these two universes aren't really two universes at all. Especially not if they're created and designed by the same God. They're two different dimensions of one universe. Like the soul and the body of one person. Or like the meaning and the words of a book, to use the analogy we used before. If you change either one, you change the other one. You can't change the meaning without changing the words, and you can't change the words without changing the meaning. In fact, the *only* way to change either one is to change the other one. The only way to change the meaning is to change the words, and the only way to change the words on the page is to change the meaning first, in your mind.

Universal common patterns to matter and spirit

And even if you call matter and spirit two different universes – which I would call a superstition – even then, if God created both of them, isn't it reasonable to expect two plays by the same playwright to have common patterns? And if it's only one play with different dimensions – the plot, the characters, the theme, the setting, the style – isn't it reasonable to expect to find a single common pattern in all the different dimensions if it's one play by one author?

'Isa: So you think human love is the "radium point" for the Theory of Everything?

Evan: I suspect it is, yes.

'Isa: Why haven't scientists looked there?

Evan: Because of their superstition of the two universes, their separation of matter and spirit.

'Isa: That "superstition," as you call it, was the origin of modern science. Once they stopped looking for spirits in the trees and souls in brains and magic in storms, they started explaining things scientifically.

Evan: Of course. But the superstitious mistake wasn't that the two dimensions are two dimensions, but that they're two universes. It's what I believe you philosophers call the "fallacy of misplaced concreteness."

Libby: I bet I know another reason why nobody looked at human love to find the Theory of Everything.

[margin note: Love as the "radium point"]

[margin note: The fallacy of misplaced concreteness]

'Isa: What's that?

Libby: That it's too obvious, too sim-ple. Sometimes, the very last place we ever look for something is the most obvious place of all. Have you ever read Edgar Allen Poe's short story, "The Purloined Letter"?

'Isa: No.

Libby: This thief has a stolen letter that's very important, very incriminating, and the police are coming into his apart-ment to search for it. They know he has it and they know he's hiding it. So he puts it right out in the middle of the table. And of course they don't look there, so they don't find it. What a great joke it would be if the key to the supreme achievement of science, the Theory of Everything, is the most "unscientific" thing in the uni-verse, the one thing no science has ever been able to explain: human love!

'Isa: I think it's not just *love*, it's *thought*, or maybe the joining of love and thought in *purpose*, or design. Any purpose has to include both mind and will, both deliberate thought and love, or at least desire. And purpose has to be the most fundamental principle of unity in any work of art that's designed by

The invisibility of the obvious

The artist's thought is imminent in the art

{80}

intelligence. To understand the art you have to understand the artist's mind and will, design and purpose, intention and desire. The artist doesn't just *express* his mind and will in the art, he *puts* his mind and will, his design and purpose, into the art. It's the *art* that has that design and purpose, not just the artist's mind and will.

Evan: That's the idea of "Intelligent design." But the problem with that idea is . . .

Libby: . . . that it's not a scientific idea but a religious idea.

Evan: No, it's not a religious idea. But it's not a scientific idea either. It's a philosophical idea. It's not a religious idea because it doesn't say there's a personal God behind it. But it's not a scientific idea because it can't be quantified and it can't be tested, it can't be verified or falsified by any possible observation or experiment.

"Intelligent design" neither religious nor scientific

'Isa: But science has discovered design everywhere. And design proves a designer. So I don't understand why "intelligent design" isn't scientific.

Evan: Because that proof isn't part of the design itself. When a culprit leaves fingerprints, the culprit isn't any one of his fingerprints. And you have to use a different kind of thinking, and a different method – not the scientific method – to make that last leap, or that last proof, from the design to the Designer.

'Isa: But there are plenty of fingerprints, don't you agree?

Evan: Oh, yes.

'Isa: So the story of the universe is an incredibly intelligent story, and an incredibly designed story.

Evan: Absolutely.

'Isa: Give us a few examples.

Evan: Why? I think you know many of these ideas already.

The Designer universe

'Isa: Because they just might trigger some new ideas.

Evan: OK. Well, it all started with the Big Bang, which was the greatest event in history because it was the event that caused or contained all other events. And the echoes of that event are all over the universe. Our own planet is still radioactive from that event. The earth's core stays hot by trillions of continuing nuclear reactions each second. And not just the core: even at the surface, even in our own bodies, atoms are still exploding.

Big Bang echoes

For instance, three million potassium atoms explode every minute in your body.

{82}

Libby: Wow. Maybe that's why I feel hot when I eat bananas.

Evan: Then there's the Anthropic Principle. The universe seems to be designed for human life to evolve, exquisitely fine-tuned to open hundreds of different tiny windows of opportunity for human life. *All* the windows have to open exactly right or human life is impossible.

The Anthropic Principle

For instance, the formation of carbon. All life depends on carbon molecules. Without carbon, no proteins, no amino acids, no vitamins, no carbohydrates, no living bodies. But carbon is made only by an extremely improbable combination of three helium atoms in the furnaces of stars, early in the universe's history, in what's called nuclear resonance. And the resonance level to form carbon is only one out of trillions of possibilities.

The near-miracle of carbon

'Isa: I read somewhere that if the energy in the Big Bang, and in the stars that it formed, had been just a tiny bit more or less, or if the temperature of the primeval fireball had been a trillionth of a degree hotter or colder, it would be physically impossible for any life to appear anywhere in all of time. Is that right?

– and of oxygen

Evan: It is. And the nuclear resonance needed to make oxygen, by combining a fourth helium atom with carbon, is even tinier. In fact, it's just about impossible.

Libby: Like the Good Book says, "with God all things are possible."

Evan: This isn't "God data." It doesn't say "God."

'Isa: But it does say "design."

Just enough curvature to space

Evan: *Everything* says "design." Even the curvature of space. It's a tiny window too, poised on the knife-edge between too much and too little. Just a tiny, tiny bit more curvature and the universe collapses into one big Black Hole. Just a tiny, tiny bit less and you get lifeless particles that can't combine.

And the history of our planet is even more chock full of data for design. For instance, when photosynthesis began, about three billion years ago, and the first bacteria and algae evolved, the "blue-green algae," their taking in of hydrogen released a lot of oxygen, and oxygen was a poison for all the life forms that had evolved so far. But there were a lot of dissolved rock minerals like iron on the surface, so the oxygen was absorbed into rust, and didn't poison the bacteria and algae. Then, about a billion years later, all the iron had turned to rust and the oxygen was free to form an oxygenated atmosphere, just in time for the life forms that needed it to breathe it.

How earth avoided oxygen poisoning

'Isa: How ironic that science can't explain the Mind that designed the only thing that science can explain.

Evan: It's often that way: only in the light of the unexplained can we explain everything. We can't look at the sun without going blind, but only in the light of the sun can we look at everything else.

The unexplained explains everything.

What I find ironic here is *us*. Here I am, a scientist, giving philosophical arguments for my scientific theory; and here you are, a philosopher, being skeptical because I'm not scientific enough.

'Isa: I'm not saying that. I have no right to say that: I'm not a scientist. I'm just being professionally agnostic, like Socrates. Because I think one of the greatest dangers in philosophy – and probably science too – is to make it a religion, or a substitute for religion – to be dogmatic about it. Even if we do find a Theory of Everything, a TOE, we've only put our little toe in the big TOE, like a

The Theory of Everything is only a little toe.

baby touching a little wave at the beach. There's a temptation to claim you've mastered the wave when you've only touched the ripple.

Evan: I completely agree with you, 'Isa. That's arrogant. But I don't think it's arrogant to believe that everything is significant, that there are signs and omens everywhere, and that all things are connected far more beautifully and simply and perfectly than we know. It's not arrogant to claim to read some of the signs. It's only arrogant to claim to read all of them.

'Isa: Isn't that what a Theory of Everything would do: claim to read all of them?

Evan: Not at all. It only claims that *each* of them is a "radium point," more or less, for *all* of them, or for the whole; in other words, that the universe is a *uni*-verse. And that's not unscientific. In fact that's the basis of all science.

'Isa: So your Theory of Everything would see something about all things, and it would be clear about that something, but it wouldn't necessarily claim to see all things clearly.

Evan: Of course not. It just means

reading some signs. It may be arrogant to claim to read *all* the signs, but it's not arrogant to claim to *read*. "Sign reading"

'Isa:　All right, what specific sign do you want to begin with? Is there one that fits this unity, or this holism, especially well?

Evan:　Let's look at synchronicity. I think that might be the unacknowledged "radium point" to the Theory of Everything.

Conversation 7: Synchronicity

Evan: I think Libby just woke up when I mentioned synchronicity.

Libby: That's because you were out of my orbit when you were talking science and philosophy. But now you're talking psychology, so now you're talking.

You mentioned synchronicity: do you mean what Jung meant by it?

Jung indefensible?

Evan: I don't think so. Not completely. In fact, I want to rescue the idea from Jung's defense of it, because I think his version is indefensible.

Libby: Well, let's see first if you mean what he meant by it. As far as I can understand him, what he meant by it was the phenomenon of two similar things – two things that share the same patterns – occurring together by apparent coincidence or chance without any discernible causal chain linking them, without either one causing the other or both being the effects of a common cause. Jung called that "a-causal parallelism."

A-causal parallelism

'Isa: I hope you don't mind if I try to clarify what Jung meant by a little philosophizing instead of psychologizing.

Libby: Go ahead.

'Isa: The problem is that he seems to be saying that some events happen without any cause at all. But that's sheer nonsense − nonsense to psychology and science and philosophy as well as to common sense. So I'm guessing that when he said some events happen without a cause, he wasn't excluding *all* causes but only one of the four kinds of cause that Aristotle distinguished: an "*efficient* cause," a cause that makes or changes or pushes around something else.

Libby: Of course. What else could he mean by a "cause"?

Efficient causes not the only kind

'Isa: Three other things. According to Aristotle, there's also a "*final* cause," a "*formal* cause" and a "*material* cause." A final cause is an end or purpose or goal. A formal cause is a form or formula or definition or pattern − an inherent structure. A material cause is a raw material, a formlessness, a potentiality for being formed by a formal cause. And according to Plato – and I think Jung was a Platonist – there's also a fifth kind of cause, which the medievals called an "*exemplary* cause," a Platonic Form, which is a kind of transcendent formal cause. That's what Jung called an "archetype." He put them into the "collective unconscious" instead of Plato's timeless higher world of Forms.

Five kinds of cause

Evan: That distinction between five kinds of causality is very helpful, 'Isa, because it defines the difference between Jung and most other scientists. Most scientists distrust final and formal causality – final causality is purposes and formal causality is essences, isn't that right, 'Isa?

'Isa: Yes.

Evan: Well, most scientists think that purposes and essences are only our inventions, not objective realities, and they explain things only by efficient causality plus material causality.

'Isa: But that's a philosophical choice, not a scientific one.

Are final and formal causes subjective?

Evan: I agree. But Jung made the opposite choice. He distrusted efficient causality and prioritized final and formal causality. Libby, do you think we're getting Jung right there?

Libby: I'm not sure if that's what he meant or not. He said simply that some events were "causeless."

'Isa: He couldn't have meant that absolutely. "Causeless events" sounds about as unscientific an idea as you can possibly come up with. It sounds like a "pop theory," that says that some events just pop into existence for no reason at all, with no cause at all. He certainly couldn't mean that. That's primitive "magical thinking."

The magical "pop" theory

Evan: I don't know whether he meant that any more than you do, and I don't really care, because I don't care about Jung, but I care about the universe; and therefore I care about whether it's got real synchronicity in it; and if synchronicity is an unreasonable idea, then I can't believe it's real. But I think synchronicity can be made much more reasonable if it's only separated from that super-strange idea of causeless events. So that's what I want to do.

'Isa: So go ahead. Do it.

Evan: I thought I just did it! But I'm not sure where to go from there.

'Isa: I think I do. I don't think we can understand synchronicity if we think

Factoring in consciousness to material events

only of relations among events in the material world. I think we have to factor in *consciousness*. And then we have to add a mutual relativity and interdependence between consciousness and its objects, between subjectivity and objectivity – I mean subjectivity and objectivity not as *attitudes* but as *realities*.

Libby: I don't understand what that means. I'm a psychologist, not a philosopher. I'm into attitudes.

'Isa: And not realities?

Libby: Just tell me where to park my attitudes.

'Isa: On the side of the road called subjectivity.

Libby: What do you mean by that?

'Isa: I mean that *all* attitudes are part of that subjective side of the road, including the attitude we call objectivity, which means the attitude of ignoring ourselves and looking only at the object.

Subject-object polarity

Libby: OK. I see. So your subject-object polarity is only the polarity between ourselves as experiencers and everything that we experience, right?

'Isa: Right.

Libby: So how does that polarity affect the theory of synchronicity?

'Isa: I think we have to look at both poles for our data, not just the object pole. And that's why the Theory of Everything needs a psychologist as much as a physicist.

Libby: OK, I guess I'm in then.

Evan: 'Isa, are you saying that the subject-object polarity is absolute?

Why the polarity can't be absolute

'Isa: No, no, the subject-object polarity can't be absolute.

Evan: Why not?

'Isa: Because it's *our* duality, and we're not the absolute. God is – remember those two pieces of wisdom from the Qur'an? So we're not the author of synchronicity, we're not the subject and designer of it. We're one of its objects, one of the things synchronized.

Libby: Ooh. That's a switch.

'Isa: But we should expect that. We should expect to be synchronized, as an author synchronizes his characters and the rest of the play – his setting and his plot and his theme and his style – into a single story.

Why we too must be "synchronized"

Libby: You mean God is the author and we are the characters and the universe is the setting.

'Isa: Of course.

Libby: And love is the plot.

'Isa: Well, I don't know about that.

Libby: Well, I do.

'Isa: The point is that if there is a single Author, we can expect everything to be synchronized. Everything, all creatures, including ourselves.

Libby: But that's just the old idea of divine providence. That's not what Jung meant by "synchronicity."

Divine providence and Jungian synchronicity

'Isa: I know that. But I'm saying that Jung's synchronicity makes more sense if we see it against the background of divine synchronicity, or divine providence. Because then you have a divine absolute that explains the relativity of subjects and objects to each other.

Libby: What does that mean, "the relativity of subjects and objects to each other"? We're simply subjects and the world is simply object, right?

Subjects to the world and objects to God

'Isa: Not absolutely, no. We are subjects to the world but we are objects to God. So we are both subjects and objects.

Libby: So we are the world's subject and God's object, the world's God and God's world.

'Isa: Not literally. We are *like* a world to God because we're His objects, and we are *like* God to the world because we are its subjects; we know it.

Even that isn't quite right, because we are *not* like God. Nothing is like God. That's where Muslim theology is the only one that's perfect and pure, and why we Muslims don't believe in any analogies to God, or images of God.

Evan: Let's not get hung up on theological correctness, or on theological disputes between Muslims and Christians about whether anything is like God, whether there are analogies to God. The point is simply that if God exists, everything is synchronized, including ourselves.

'Isa: Well, of course. All that means is that everything is subject to God's mind and will, God's providence. And that's nothing *new*. If God exists, we can *expect* everything to be synchronized, including us and the universe. And we can also expect that we can't synchronize the Author with anything else, because the Synchronizer can't be one of the things synchronized. That's why divine providence can't be not a *scientific* idea at all: because it's not objectifiable to us. We're part of it, not outside it, as God is

Why Providence is not a scientific idea

Evan: And it's also not scientific because it's not falsifiable, not refutable, even in principle. No matter what happens, a believer would say that was part of divine providence. There's no empirical data open to science that can ever prove it or disprove it.

Libby: But Jung's synchronicity *is* a scientific theory for him. Because he didn't bring God into it, he just looked at the data. God may really be there behind the data, like a weaver behind a tapestry; but the tapestry is the only data we have.

The universe like a tapestry

Evan: The tapestry is the universe, you mean?

Libby: Yes. The universe is like a tapestry. Every thread in the tapestry is relative to every other one, as everything in the universe is relative to everything else in the universe.

'Isa: But that's nothing new either, and nothing controversial. What is there that's new and controversial in Jung's theory of synchronicity that might be a door to the Theory of Everything?

Evan: What's new in Jung is not the idea of interdependence, but the lack of efficient causality in that interdependence.

{96}

'Isa: When he talked about interdependence, did he mean interdependence between physical events?

Libby: Yes, and also between mental events, and also interdependence between physical events and mental events.

Evan: What do you mean by "mental events"?

Libby: States of our psyche. Ideas, expectations, intuitions, images, moods, dreams, visions, trances, out-of-body experiences, meditation, anything.

Evan: Even science?

Libby: Even science.

'Isa: So what, exactly, did Jung claim was true about "synchronicity"?

Libby: He discovered frequent connections that couldn't be explained by efficient causality. Some of these were connections between two physical events separated too much by space and time for there to be efficient causality between them. Some of them were mental events that had no conscious mental connections between them, like memories of things you had never experienced. And some of them were connections between mental events and physical events: some people seemed to *think* things into existence.

Evidence for synchronicity

'Isa: I'd like to go over what the different philosophers say about these cases, if you don't mind, so that I can understand which philosophical school Jung fits into.

Evan, Libby: Go ahead.

Not materialism

'Isa: Let's take materialism first. Materialists would say that all events are material and all causality is material. If they admit the mental as distinct from the material at all, they say it's always an effect, not a cause, like the puff of smoke that comes out the tailpipe of your car — that's called "epiphenomenalism."

Libby: Jung was certainly not a materialist.

Not immaterialism

'Isa: A second possibility is idealism. Idealists, or immaterialists, would say all events are mental and all causality is mental. They say that matter is a projection of mind — usually not *our* mind but some kind of divine mind or cosmic mind. So matter is either wholly within mind, like dreams, or at least causally dependent on mind, as the images on a movie screen are dependent on the projecting machine.

Libby: Jung was not an idealist either, at least not that kind of idealist. Although

Not dualism he's a lot closer to idealism than to materialism.

'Isa: Then there's a third view, dualism, which says there's two-way causality: from mind to matter and from matter to mind. That's much more commonsensical. But that has trouble explaining how either of the two kinds of causality *between* the two can exist. How can a spirit push the buttons of a machine? And how can a machine push a spirit around?

Libby: That's easy. It only happens in us, because we're a psycho-somatic unity. We're not ghosts in machines but something like a work of art, like a poem or a symphony. Works of art are material things, like us, but the meaning and beauty of the things isn't material. It's another *dimension.* And as you said before, you can't change one dimension without changing the other. You can't change the meaning of a poem without changing the words and you can't change the words without changing the meaning.

'Isa: That's commonsensical, all right. But that's not dualism. That's Aristotle's "hylomorphism." That's a fourth position. But that's not Jung either, is it? Because that doesn't allow for Jung's synchronicity. I'm trying to find the philosophical presuppositions of his idea

Hylo-morphism?

of synchronicity, at least the philosophical anthropology behind it.

Libby: Synchronicity isn't a theory about the relation between matter and spirit. It's a theory about the relation between two events, whether the two events are both physical, or both spiritual, or one of each. It means another kind of connection between two events, one that we haven't mentioned yet. The connection is neither material nor mental but it's a connection by a common *pattern*.

'Isa: Aristotle would call that "formal causality." Like two dogs having the same essential form, or essential nature. But that's not controversial either. I thought Jung's idea was something new and controversial.

Evan: It is. In fact, it's so new and so controversial that many people think it's crazy. Let me explain it the way Rupert Sheldrake did . . .

Rupert Sheldrake's "morphic fields"

'Isa: Who's that?

Evan: He was an Englishman, an oddball sort of biological scientist. He formulated the principle of synchronicity this way: he said that if something new happens once, it will happen again even without any conscious copying, like memory, or any physical causing, like Xerox machines. He explained that by a strange-sounding hypothesis: a "morphic field" that was generated or caused by repetition, and which also caused repetition, or at least increased the likelihood of repetition.

For instance, glycerin was never observed to form crystals. Forty years of observation and not one case ever appeared of glycerin forming crystals. Then one day a dram of glycerine began to crystallize en route from Vienna to London. Shortly after that happened, another batch of glycerin, untouched by the first one, did the same.

Testing the theory by experiment

'Isa: Did anybody confirm the theory by replicating that data?

Evan: Yes.

'Isa: With glycerin?

Evan: No, with another kind of pattern. This one involved minds. An English TV station made two paintings of random patterns. On the first one they hid the figure of a woman wearing a hat. On the second one they hid the figure of a man with a mustache. It was almost impossible to see those hidden figures clearly with ordinary vision. *Before* the TV program went on, a group of people was asked to identify what they saw in the two paintings. Then, *during* the TV show, the secret of the second painting was revealed: the man with the mustache, but not the woman with the hat. Once it was revealed, everybody noticed it. Then, *after* the show, a second group of people, who didn't see the show, was asked to identify what they saw in the two paintings. The second group did a far better job identifying the man with the mustache, but not the woman with the hat.

'Isa: So what is that supposed to demonstrate?

Evan: That when one group becomes aware of something, others do too, even if the two groups don't meet. That's the data. And the hypothesis that explains it is that the new pattern spontaneously repeats, finds a second place to occur, without any efficient causality connecting the first and second occurrences.

Subconscious mental telepathy?

'Isa: I'd explain that by a subconscious mental telepathy, and that's a form of efficient causality. I still don't see why Jung disbelieved in efficient causality.

Evan: The experiment we talked about before is another example of synchronicity. The one where you start with a pair of joined subatomic particles, sort of like Siamese twins, you split them apart and send them off in opposite directions in space, so that they're no longer connected physically, and then if you do things to either one of them – zap it with a beam of energy – the other one will react as it it's being zapped in exactly the same way. Like two Siamese twins being separated and still having mental telepathy with each other even if they're on opposite sides of the earth.

'Isa: But subatomic particles have no mental telepathy. They have no mental life at all.

Evan: That's exactly the point. There's no efficient causality, mental or physical. Yet the pattern replicates.

Libby: Like a sound wave.

Evan: Like any kind of wave. Because that's the fundamental pattern of all energy, the wave. That's the form of all forms. So maybe that's the secret of synchronicity.

Libby: Then let's talk about waves. That's something I know about.

Telepathy among subatomic particles?

Waves, the form of forms

Conversation 8: Waves

[Editor's comments: This dialog is more relaxed and conversational than the others. It wanders off onto tangents more, and tries to logically prove less, than the others. There is nothing a tape recorder can do about that, even with editing. I included it because of the intrinsic interest of its topics, even though they are far from being connected with each other with adequate logic.]

Why are we fascinated with waves?

Libby: I've always been fascinated with waves – and with our fascination with them. And I think I've figured it out: I think we're fascinated with them because we know, unconsciously, that they show us the two fundamental realities of the universe, matter and energy. We know more than we know, you know.

'Isa: I know. And waves also show us that great philosophical puzzle of what

{104}

happens when an irresistible force meets an immovable object.

The irresistible force vs. the immovable object

Libby: The waves always win, don't they? They never stop crashing on the rocks, but the rocks stop being rocks and eventually turn into sand.

'Isa: Do you think that shows you that there *is* no immovable object but there is an irresistible force?

Force more fundamental than objects

Libby: It shows that force is more fundamental than objects.

'Isa: But even the waves will stop at some time, billions of years from now.

Libby: But the waves still show us that force is more fundamental than objects, that energy is more fundamental than matter. And that's true scientifically, isn't it, Evan?

Evan: Yes, it is. When energy is transformed into matter, it "solidifies" into matter, so to speak; but when matter is transformed into energy, in nuclear fission or fusion, the energy is "released."

Energy more fundamental than matter

Libby: So the energy is like the prisoner and the matter is like his prison cell.

Evan: That's a nice poetic way of saying it, yes. Paradoxically, matter is not made of matter. Matter is made of energy. Energy is the reality of matter.

What is matter made of?

Now this energy, this fundamental reality, has a pattern, a form. And that fundamental form of that fundamental reality is the wave.

'Isa: That's true of matter, but what about thought? That's a form of energy too, but it's not just material energy.

Thought comes in waves too.

Evan: Thought comes in waves too. We speak not only of "light waves" and "sound waves" and "gravity waves" but also of "brain waves."

'Isa: But remember what we said about mind and brain. The brains of corpses don't give out any "brain waves" even though the brain is still there, because the soul is gone. But are there *thought* waves too, and not just "brain waves"? Are there soul waves?

Libby: Emotion certainly comes in waves.

'Isa: How could you tell unless you saw their material manifestation in brain waves?

Evan: We don't have to get into the big philosophical question of the relation between matter and spirit now. We did that before. Let's just look at the fundamental wave pattern of everything that we do see.

'Isa: OK.

Evan: A wave is what happens when you put energy into time. Energy plus time equals a wave.

Energy + time = waves

'Isa: But what is time?

Libby: Congratulations, 'Isa. You steered clear of philosophical questions for a whole ten seconds there.

Evan: No, that's a scientific question too. And I think Plato's famous philosophical definition of time is more scientific than people think it is, if only we think of a wave. Plato defined time as "*the moving image of eternity.*" Isn't that right, 'Isa?

'Isa: Yes.

Evan: And a wave is *a moving image of time.* A wave is time made visible by being imaged in *space.*

Waves as time made spatially visible

'Isa: So time is the image of eternity and space is the image of time.

Libby: That's too abstract for me. But I like Plato's definition of time.

'Isa: Why?

Libby: Because it's great poetry.

'Isa: That's not a good reason to accept a definition!

Libby: It is here. Because it *works.* And it works for poetry for the same reason it works for science: *because of waves.*

'Isa: What do you mean?

Libby: A wave of the sea is a moving image of the sea, and the sea is like eternity.

'Isa: But the sea is not really changeless.

Libby: Of course not. But it's a natural poetic *image* of changelessness, or eternity. A Jungian archetype. And it's also dynamic at the same time. It pumps out waves because it's a sea of *energy*.

Evan: Actually, it's not the sea itself but the wind that raises waves.

Libby: But it still works as an image. It's a paradoxical union of changelessness and dynamism. It makes the sea a natural image of eternity.

Evan: Yes. It's both static and dynamic, both changeless and changing.

'Isa: How is it changeless?

Evan: Things change *in* it but *it* doesn't change because there's no place or time outside of it for it to move to. It's the sum of all space and time.

But nothing *in* the universe is unchanging. Everything acts. Even the rock that just sits there is changing. It only seems to be unchanging to our limited senses. Wait long enough and you'll see

Why is the sea a natural image of eternity?

Changelessness and dynamism united

it change to sand. Because the waves wear all the rocks away. That's an image of everything that happens in the universe.

'Isa: So the things in the universe are all like that rock.

Evan: Yes. They're not mere collections of hard, unchanging particles, as the old materialistic version of the atomic theory said.

No hard, unchanging particles

'Isa: And they're also not dreams or illusions of our minds, as idealist philosophy says. And they're not insubstantial emptiness, as Buddhist philosophy says. And they're not dreams in the mind of God, or God Himself in disguise, as Hindu philosophy says.

Evan: No. They're waves. Everything comes in waves.

Libby: So the universe is like the sea, and the life of the sea is both active and changeless, like the life of God.

'Isa: *You* say "like the life of God." But I would say that nothing is like God.

Libby: First philosophy, now theology. You can't stay in pure science long, 'Isa.

'Isa: Thanks for the compliment.

Libby: I didn't mean it as a compliment.

'Isa: I know.

Libby: You know, I love these trialogs with you, 'Isa, a lot better than dialogs, because they let me ignore you for a minute and talk to Evan instead. Hey, Evan, what about particles? Isn't *that* the form of matter?

Waves vs. particles

Evan: Insofar as we distinguish matter from energy, yes. But all particles are related to all other particles in a single continuum, the space-time continuum that we call the universe. And that universe is governed by only a few fundamental forces. And the one that impacts us most directly is gravity. And gravity also comes in waves, "gravity waves." And of course radioactivity and electromagnetic energy also come in waves.

'Isa: What about light? That's got a special place in the universe, doesn't it? And that comes in waves too.

The anomaly of light

Evan: Yes. Light is special because the speed of light is the universal constant, the one absolute barrier. Nothing can move faster than light. But light is not only waves but also particles. It's also the only thing that's both wave and particle.

'Isa: Does anybody have an explanation for that?

Evan: Not a simple one.

'Isa: I do.

Libby: Well, Einstein, don't keep us in the dark.

'Isa: It's not a scientific explanation, but it's a philosophical one. I'd say that it's because light is the thing that's the closest to being both energy and matter at once. It's that form of matter which most resembles energy, or that form of energy that most resembles matter. And since matter is made of particles and energy is made of waves, light is both particles and waves.

Light: matter or energy?

Evan: Interesting explanation, 'Isa. Do you also have an explanation for why energy is more fundamental than matter?

'Isa: That's easy . . .

Libby: That's our 'Isa! And in another week or so, he's going to invent invisibility machines and antigravity machines and time machines. So what's your "easy" explanation?

'Isa: Energy is more fundamental than matter because it's more universal. It includes spiritual energy as well as physical energy. But matter doesn't include "spiritual matter" as well as physical matter. All matter is physical.

Libby: So that's why waves are more fundamental than particles?

The priority of waves over particles

'Isa: That too, yes.

Evan: And therefore a Universal Wave Theory would be a greater discovery than Universal Gravitation: it's more universal. It would explain spiritual energy as well as physical energy, and it would unify the two.

Libby: So it would connect things like the rise and fall of love and aggression and joy and despair with the rise and fall of life and tides and menstrual cycles?

Evan: Yes. And maybe it would also explain something in theology: why Adam and Eve are two and yet one; why "Adam" means both "mankind" and "the male half of mankind"; and why Eve was taken out of Adam, like nuclear fission, and why marriage is like nuclear fusion.

Marriage and nuclear fusion

Libby: Wow. That sounds weird. I never heard anybody make that connection before. But that's either poetry or theology. How can it be physics? I thought physics was mathematical.

Evan: And that's another dualism that would have to be bridged. Modern physics *is* mathematical. It's ruthlessly quantified. It's called "quantum physics," after all, and that means its only language is digital, zero-sum, either/or.

{112}

'Isa: If visible things are ultimately made of those quantum leaps, how can we talk about visible things in non-quantitative language then?

Evan: Because particles are unlike anything visible. They're like numbers: absolutely discrete. Numbers are the only things that are absolutely discrete.

Only numbers and particles are discrete.

'Isa: Isn't that a good reason to think that numbers, and maybe even the particles that we can't talk about except quantitatively, are only projections of our digital consciousness, rather than things-in-themselves, objective realities?

Evan: No, I don't think it is. But I don't want to go into that philosophical question here.

Libby: I think we should call the Theory of Everything "the Universal Wave Theory," since everything comes in waves.

"The universal wave theory"

'Isa: Especially light. Light was the first thing created, and the standard and measure of all motion. And it comes in waves.

1. light

Libby: And water too, which was the second thing created.

2. water

Evan: I think in the Bible "light" means not only literal light but also a symbol for energy, and "water" or "the waters" means not only H_2O but also a symbol for matter.

3. sound

Libby: And sound comes in waves too. And the sound the whole universe makes, according to old Pythagoras, is "the music of the spheres."

4. justice

'Isa: Plato called that "justice," and he connected it to music. You know,

5. music

there's more about music than about politics in Plato's *Republic*.

Libby: As the poet said, "by justice the stars are strong."

6. time

Evan: And don't forget time. That also comes in waves.

'Isa: Newton's "absolute time" is just one-dimensional, like a line, right? But Einstein's "relative time" curves into a second dimension like a wave, right?

Evan: You could say that. Einstein proved that time is relative to motion rather than motion being relative to time, as Newton had thought. Motion measures time rather than time measuring motion.

'Isa: So the cosmic music measures time rather than time measuring the music.

Evan: That's right. This music *makes* time, and everything that happens is a note in this music.

'Isa: So whatever we do is a note in this music.

Evan: Yes.

'Isa: So what we do makes life, and life makes time.

Evan: Yes, and the music makes time *as it moves*. That's why there's no Newtonian absolute time. Time is a product of motion, of the music, of the waves.

Libby: Now I see it: that's why all of life is like surfing.

'Isa: I knew you'd get to that.

Libby: Since time is a product of motion, it's like the scent thrown off by a running animal.

Evan: That's a very poetic way of putting it.

Libby: But it's true, isn't it? It says the same thing as the other image, the image of music. Both are images of waves, whether it's time waves or sound waves – I mean music waves.

'Isa: Go over the music image again. Why is everything music?

Why everything is music

Libby: Everything in the universe makes music, because everything vibrates, like a string, and generates waves of energy, and those waves make a music. Everything *sings*, at its own frequency.

People too. They have "vibes," vibrations. Their souls give off vibrations.

This explains evil.

'Isa: And that would explain why man alone can be evil. Because of free will, soul vibrations are the only vibrations in the universe that can be bad, can be disharmonious.

Libby: Evan, tell us some scientific data about waves. Like what's the formula for them?

The energy in a wave

Evan: Well, there's a simple formula for the energy in a water wave, in pounds per square foot. It's "$E = WLH^2$," where E is energy, W is the weight of a cubic foot of water, or 64 lbs., and L is the length of the wave, the length of the trough between two waves, and H is the height of the wave. So a 12-foot wave coming 10 seconds before the next one would have 295 tons of energy per square foot.

How big can waves get?

Libby: What was the biggest wave ever recorded?

Evan: One in Lituya Bay, Alaska, off Gilbert Inlet. It was caused by a rock mass of 90 million tons dropping off the cliff into the sea.

Libby: Did anyone live to see it?

Evan: No.

Libby: Then how could they measure it?

Evan: Because the destruction of life that came from that wave reached a height of over 1,700 feet. Every blade of grass and every bush and tree up to 1,720 feet was totally destroyed.

Libby: Wow.

Evan: And at Tillamook Rock Light in Oregon a wave once tossed a 135-pound boulder through the roof of a beacon that stood 139 feet above high water – *from above.*

'Isa: You seem to be an expert in wave history, Evan. What's the strongest recorded wave ever?

Evan: I think it's the one in Wick, Scotland, in 1872. A single wave washed away a whole block of concrete at the end of a breakwater that weighed 2,700,000 pounds. The pressure was calculated at 4,000 pounds per square foot.

'Isa: How high can the pressure go?

Evan: It can go as high as 17,000 pounds per square foot.

'Isa: How can it go that high?

Evan: If the wave traps enough air and compresses it and then releases it when it bursts.

Libby: That's really moving!

Evan: But the water in a wave doesn't really move forward, the way it seems to.

Libby: Why?

Evan: Because if it did, the ocean would soon empty out and flood the land. The ocean would soon become dry and the dry land wet.

Libby: But when you throw a stone into a pool, the waves spread out away from the stone.

Evan: But the center doesn't empty out. The pool doesn't become a dry dough-nut. It's the form that moves, not the matter.

'Isa: And it's like that with us too.

Libby, Evan: What do you mean?

'Isa: It's the form that moves, and acts, and lives, and dies, and survives death, but not the matter. I mean it's the soul. That's our form. And it gets new matter, new atoms, every seven years in every part of the body except the brain. Isn't that right, Evan?

Evan: Yes.

'Isa: So we're waves too, with a seven-year fetch.

Libby: Maybe that explains "the seven-year itch."

Evan: And when a wave touches you,

Why water waves don't move

The form moves, not the water

We are waves.

it's the whole sea touching you. The wave is like its hand. When I touch you with my hand, it's not just my hand that touches you, it's *me*. So when we're touched by a wave, it's not just the wave but the whole sea waving at us.

And the water in that wave that splashed on you in Massachusetts came from the Amazon and the Antarctic. Because all water is interchanged in the global ecosystem. It's a closed system, like a circulatory system. A mystic might call it a hydrogenated communion of saints.

Libby: How does the circulation happen?

Evan: It depends on two things: time and space. And there's plenty of both for the sea. It takes an average water molecule in a wave about 5,000 years to traverse all the oceans of the earth and return home. Water is a world traveler.

Libby: So I can say, "Hi, Amazon" to the foam deposited on my beach.

'Isa: But how has this gotten us closer to our Universal Wave Theory?

Evan: I don't know, exactly. But it explains our fascination with waves.

Libby: And it sort of smells right, doesn't it?

The whole sea "waves" at us.

"The hydrogenated communion of saints"

A 5,000-year trip around the world

Conversation 9: Holism

Evan: That doesn't make it scientific, you know: the mere fact that it "smells" right!

'Isa: Wait a minute: smells exist. Literally. And their objects exist. Literally. And science is about everything that exists in the universe.

Libby: Some of the objects of smell aren't literal, you know. There are some people who can literally smell death. In any case, *I* didn't mean "smell" literally.

Smelling as analogous to intuition

'Isa: I know that. You used "smelling" instead of "seeing" as an analogy for an intuition as distinct from definitions and arguments, right?

Libby: Yes. And we just said that intuition has to count too, and has to be used too, for a Theory of Everything.

Evan: That's true, but it's far too vague and sloppy to be useful scientifically.

We can't just sit here and spout our immediate intuitions and think we've made any progress. We've got to be rational too.

'Isa: And once the Theory of Everything is stated, in whatever form, "being rational" has to mean being *critical*: judging it, trying to prove it or disprove it.

But the first thing that "being rational" has to mean to us now, at the beginning of our search, is the need to give a rational *basis* for the search, giving a reason for the hope that such a theory can ever be found. That's what we can do now, I think, even without a lot of scientific data and a lot of mathematics.

The need for a critical basis for the search for the Theory of Everything

Evan: So what would that basis be?

'Isa: The unity of the universe. If it really is a *uni*-verse, then everything in it must be connected, in some way. We already know some of those ways, like the laws of physics – things like gravity – and the laws of psychology – things like motivation. But there's got to be many more ways things are connected that we don't know, especially ways matter and mind are connected.

All things connected

Libby: What ways did you have in mind?

'Isa: If I had them in mind, they'd

be ways I know already, wouldn't they?

Even ESP

Libby: I thought you meant things like ESP and clairvoyance and out-of-body experiences, and mystical experiences.

'Isa: That's part of it, if that really happens.

Two Societies for Psychical Research

Evan: And it apparently does. There's abundant evidence for it. Of course a lot of it is fake, but a lot of it isn't. The Society for Psychical Research has been collecting evidence of it for over a century, and their methods are stringently scientific – there are two of them, one in England and one in America.

Libby: But what we really *know* about that whole area is only the tiniest little hints, like the little foamy bubbles from a great wave that just broke on the sand.

Evan: That's true. And the most important thing we don't know, I think, is just how much of the data is really data.

'Isa: How can data not be data?

Why evidence for ESP is only anecdotal

Evan: The evidence is anecdotal, not scientific. There aren't any good replicated experiments. People who have these unusual powers are anomalies, and they can't be duplicated. They can't teach others how to do it. And their psychic powers, or whatever you want to call them, can't be controlled and repeated at will, as ordinary powers of ordinary consciousness can, like breathing or singing or calculating. These extraordinary phenomena "just happen," when these people "let go."

Libby: But everything that happens, happens, whether the scientific method can take account of it or not. *We're* not scientific either, *we're* "anecdotal," because we're individuals who can't be replicated. But we're real.

Why *we* are "anectotal"

'Isa: Suppose you had an identical twin. Or a clone. Why wouldn't that replicate you?

Libby: Because even if my clone and I thought the same thoughts, my thoughts would all be *my* thoughts and not his thoughts.

'Isa: That's a good answer.

Libby: Think of Tweedledum and Tweedledee. An outsider couldn't see any difference between the two of them, but Tweedledum would see it. In fact, Tweedledum would see that there's a *total* difference between him and Tweedledee. Not one of the parts of Tweedledee is a part of Tweedledum: not one toe or one hair, and not one thought.

Tweedledum and Tweedledee

{123}

Evan: Now what do you think that tells us about the universe?

Libby: The universe includes everything that happens, everything in time. And anomalies and singularities happen too. So a Theory of Everything would have to take account of anomalies and singularities too.

How to include anomalies?

Evan: But a scientific theory, by definition, can't do that. It requires replication. If you can't repeat a phenomenon, you can't control it. And if you can't control it, you can't repeat it at will.

Libby: That's why the Theory of Everything can't be just a "left-brain" theory. Somehow it has to use "right-brain" intuition, and maybe even "mystical" intuition, too.

Evan: But how? That's never been done before.

Libby: Surfers do it on every wave.

'Isa: Do what? Find the Theory of Everything? Why haven't you shared it with the rest of the world then?

Surfing gets our brains together.

Libby: It's kind of hard to write on a surfboard. No, silly, we don't find the Theory of Everything. But maybe we find the *method* for finding it. We get our brains together.

{124}

'Isa: And that's why you can get the universe together?

Libby: Right on, man. Now *you're* gettin' it together.

'Isa: Let's be serious for a moment, OK? We started this conversation by talking about the unity of the universe as the *foundation* for the Theory of Everything. Then we drifted off into one *application* of that principle: that the theory would have to account for anomalies like psychic phenomena. And then we started to ask how that could be done, what *method* would transcend the scientific method, which can't, in principle, explain these things. Which of those three questions should we focus on?
We can't do all three at once.

Libby: Not if we confine ourselves to analysis, and separations, and definitions, we can't. But I thought we just agreed that we have to transcend that.

'Isa: Not in procedure. We can "go mystical" but we can't *confuse* things.

Libby: What things?

'Isa: We're thinking about the aspects of the universe that intuition reveals – that's the first-order question – and we're thinking about integrating intuition

First-, second-, third-, and fourth-order questions

{125}

with analysis, as a way of understanding the universe – that's the second-order question – and we're thinking about integrating intuitive *methods* with analytical methods – that's the third-order question – but *that* thinking-about, the thinking about the methods of thinking – the fourth-order question – that has to be clear and logical, I think.

Libby: I don't agree.

'Isa: Why not?

Libby: It's not that way on a wave. That's where I do my best thinking.

'Isa: If you're right, I guess I just don't know how to do that.

How to transcend logic

Libby: Go get a wetsuit and I'll show you.

'Isa: No, I mean I don't know how to argue in any other way than logically, whether I'm arguing about the universe, or ways of knowing it, or ways of combining ways of knowing it.

Libby: Poor boy!

Evan: Hey, you two, we've been moving farther and farther away from the universe, and now we're four steps removed from it, in "fourth-order questions." Let's get back to the first-order questions, shall we? Let's test the idea that just a few minutes ago 'Isa identified as the philosophical foundation for the Theory of Everything, the unity of the universe, and its corollary that everything that happens is connected with everything else.

'Isa & Libby: OK.

Evan: Here's a quotation I copied from Chesterton. It challenges us to think about connectedness in a new way that science hasn't yet understood. It's about magic, which is a very *old* way of thinking about connectedness. I wonder whether this very old way, this very unscientific way, might not point to the new way, the super-scientific way, that we're looking for. That would be quite a paradox, wouldn't it? Here it is:

"Suppose somebody in a story says 'Pluck this flower and a princess will die in a castle beyond the sea.' We do not know why something stirs in the subconsciousness, or why what is impossible seems almost inevitable. Suppose we read 'And in the hour when the king extinguished the candle his ships were wrecked far away on the coast of Hebrides.' We do not know why the imagination has accepted that image before the reason can reject it, or why such correspondences

The truth in myth and 'magic': connectedness

seem really to correspond to something in the soul. Very deep things in our nature, some dim sense of the dependence of great things upon small, some dark suggestion that the things nearest to us stretch far beyond our power, some sacramental feeling of the magic in material substances . . ."

Libby: He's right. He's absolutely right – How did he know that? He's a *man*.

Evan: How do you know he's right, Libby?

Libby: Because I know the pulse in the sea and the pulse in my heart, and they're the same pulse. Because I know the pulse in the sea *by* the pulse in my heart. And I know there's a connection between the wave's longing to break free of gravity and fly up into the sky just before it breaks, and my heart's longing to leap over the sea when I kick out of a wave on my shortboard.

Evan: I'm not a surfer, but I can feel that longing too, the longing to fly, or just to leap over rocks like a goat.

Libby: What's going on there? Two bloodstreams are being pumped by the same heart. That's why the pulse is the same.

Connecting our and nature's pulses and longings

'Isa: Do you mean the two blood-streams are the outer reality and the inner reality, the physical and the psychological, the objective and the subjective, what you sense with your body and what you sense with your soul?

Libby: I think so.

'Isa: Then what is the heart that pumps both?

Libby: Maybe it's God.

Evan: Then we're doomed.

Libby: I know you're a Calvinist, Evan, but do you always say "doom" when you say "God"?

Evan: I don't mean it that way. I mean we're doomed to fail in our quest for the Theory of Everything if the only answer is God. Because God can't be in the equation, God can't be a part of the equation, just as God will never be found in a laboratory. God is transcendent. God is not inside the universe.

'Isa: Yes, but what other answer could there possibly be? I think God *must* be the only possible answer that combines the two very different halves of the data, just as God is the only possible answer that combines the data of free choice and fate.

> Is God the heart that pumps the universe?

> God *can't* be the answer

> God *must* be the answer

Libby: I don't see the close parallel.

Story as the solution to the puzzle of fate and free will

'Isa: Here are two factors that are both real, both part of the universe, part of everybody's life and experience. Every story ever told has both factors in it. If there's no free choice, it's not a story at all. And if there's no destiny, no fate, then it's also not a story, just a jumble of accidental factoids falling into each other. So a Theory of Everything has to connect free choice and fate somehow.

Libby: That assumes, of course, that both are real.

'Isa: Yes. Two cheap ways of solving the problem are to deny either of those two halves of our data. Determinists deny free will and atheists deny fate, and atheistic determinists deny both. That's why they never write good stories.

Now assuming that we don't deny either half of the data, and assuming that a complete theory or philosophy has to combine them somehow, and assuming that the story of our lives does in fact combine them, I see only one way to do it, and that's by a transcendent God. Because the only good analogy we have for the strange stories of our lives, which combine both fate and free choice, is the stories we ourselves invent. And we, the storytellers, are transcendent to the stories we tell. Shakespeare isn't part of Hamlet. And Shakespeare is the only explanation that connects Hamlet's fate and Hamlet's free choices, as the common cause of both. So a transcendent God would have to be the only thing that can connect our free choices and our fates.

The Shakespeare analogy

Evan: Well, maybe not. Maybe that's not necessarily the *only* thing. You're making a logical mistake, 'Isa. You're *arguing* from an analogy.

'Isa: You're right. I am. But it seems like the best analogy, doesn't it?

Evan: Yes, I don't think a transcendent God, a transcendent Unifier of the universe, has to exclude an *immanent* unifier too. God uses immanent causes, second causes, natural causes. There could be a divine fingerprint, so to speak, *in* the universe. So even though the Theory of Everything can't include God as one of its ingredients, it could include His universal fingerprints.

The immanent unifier: the divine fingerprint

You see, 'Isa, you were thinking of God as a merely extrinsic cause, like a puppeteer. I was thinking of God as an artist. And the mind of the artist is in some

God's presence artistic

sense *in* his art, though it's not *confined* to his art or limited to his art.

More than that, even: it's a kind of *sacramental* presence. It's what the Catholics believe about their sacraments: the bread and wine on the altar are obviously bread and wine, but they are also God, God's body.

'Isa: That's blasphemous and ridiculous!

Evan: I understand how it has to seem blasphemous to you as a Muslim. And it should seem blasphemous to Libby and me as Protestant Christians too if we don't believe it: worshipping wine and bread as if it was God – that's idolatry.

'Isa: Of course, if what Catholics believe *is* true, then *you're* as wrong as you thought *they* were. There's no mediating that either/or, logically.

Evan: My point is not whether sacramentalism is true or not theologically. My point is that it's an analogy to the universe. A sacramental universe is something like a baby experiencing its mother's love in nursing.

'Isa: That's fine for a poet but not for a scientist or even a philosopher.

God's presence sacramental?

The mother-baby analogy

Evan: No, I think it's good philosophy. Look here, love is an immaterial act
of the soul, right?

'Isa: Right.

Evan: And the mother's milk, and the
mother's breast, and the mother's body,
and the mother's caressing hands are all
material, physical things, right?

'Isa: Right. And so is the baby's
mouth and the baby's body.

Evan: Now what is the relationship
between the mother's love and the milk
that goes from the mother's body into the
baby's body?

'Isa: The milk is the *effect* of the
mother's love and it's the *cause* of the baby's
immediate pleasure and eventual health.

Evan: Yes, it is that, but it's more
than that, I think. I think the milk *is* the
mother's love. The love comes to the baby
immediately, *as milk*. The milk isn't just
the product, the effect. That's too external.

The causality more than extrinsic

It's like an old hymn we sing in church:

Thy bountiful care what tongue can recite?
It breathes in the air; it shines in the light;
It streams from the hills; it descends to the plain;
And sweetly distills in the dew and the rain.

Look at the grammar there: God's care, God's love, which is spiritual and not made of molecules, is the immediate subject of the verbs. IT breathes in the air. IT shines in the light. IT streams from the hills. It's not just an *effect* of God's love, it *is* God's love incarnate.

'Isa: We Muslims don't believe in the Incarnation.

Evan: I know.

Libby: Why are we having this theological argument? I thought we were doing science.

Evan: Because I think 'Isa's theology may impede his science.

'Isa: What? Are you saying that only Christians can ever find the Theory of Everything?

Evan: No, but I'm saying that if there is a God, and He is the ultimate unifier, then we have to be open to the idea that this ultimate unifier is immanent as well as transcendent – though of course our Theory of Everything will only find His universal fingerprint, so to speak, or the underside of His tapestry, to change the metaphor.

'Isa: I can admit that in a sense. The *will* of God is in all things, certainly. A

Nature as divine love incarnate

hadith of Muhammad says: Wherever you turn, there is the Face of Allah.

God's *will* also intrinsic

Evan: And the will of God is what makes God's presence intrinsic; that's what makes the universe more like a play than a puppet show. The will of the puppeteer simply pulls the strings of all the puppets, but the will of the dramatist is *in* the free choices of his characters even though some of them are evil and seem to oppose the good will of the author and of the good characters.

'Isa: Are you saying that the will of the author is double, then?

Evan: What do you mean?

'Isa: The author wills that the villain *not* choose evil, and yet he also wills that the villain *does* choose evil, because that's part of the story.

Does God will evil?

Evan: Yes.

'Isa: That won't work theologically. God can't have two wills that contradict each other.

Does God have two wills?

Evan: I agree. So one will has to be subordinate to the other.

'Isa: So freedom has to be subordinate to fate.

Libby: No way. I say fate has to be subordinate to freedom.

Evan: But we don't have to solve that theological problem here. All we're looking for is the universal divine fingerprint in the story of the universe that we've called the Theory of Everything.

'Isa & Libby: OK.

Evan: And I think that unity of the universe is more intimate to it than the unity of an extrinsic cause to its effects, like a puppeteer's will to his puppets. So even if the unity of the universe *is* rooted in the will of God, it's not *only* that. God put more unity *into* the universe than mere obedience to His will.

'Isa: I disagree. There *is* no greater unity than that, in Muslim theology.

Evan: OK, then, let's just say God put more unity into the universe than an extrinsic unity. He also put into it an intrinsic unity, a mind unity, a plan, a pattern. Even if His will is the extrinsic efficient cause of the universe, His mind also invented all the formal causes for the universe.

'Isa: I accept that.

Evan: So we can still search for the formula, the form.

Libby: But that isn't just not just a

Extrinsic unity = power

Intrinsic unity = mind

mathematical formula. Because that's only the analytic half, right?

Evan: Right.

'Isa: What is it, then?

Libby: I think it's like the point of a great joke.

The unity of the universe is the point of a great joke.

Evan: So the content of the joke is like the matter, all the matter and energy in the universe; and the point of the joke, the joke of the joke, is the form?

Libby: Yeah.

Evan: So scientists haven't found it yet because they don't have a big enough sense of humor?

Libby: Yeah, I like that.

'Isa: May I point out that your likes and dislikes don't determine the universe?

Libby: You may. And I may also ignore it.

Evan: Seriously, our likes and dislikes are also part of the universe, so they are relevant. They are part of the data.

'Isa: But she's right: a sense of humor might be something like a sense of poetry or a sense of music: the missing center. There's a "point" to a poem, and the point is in all the words but also transcends them. The whole is not just the

A sense of humor a missing element

sum of the parts. And there's a point to a picture, and to a piece of music, that permeates all the parts and makes it a whole. It answers the question: Why are these brush strokes or these notes here, in this order, rather than others? What did the artist *mean?* But it's hard to formulate the answer to that question in any other way than just the picture itself, and it's even harder to formulate the answer to the question of what a piece of music "means" in any other way than the music itself. In fact, it's probably impossible.

The non-formula-bility of t he *point* of a work of art

Libby: So maybe the whole point of the universe is just the universe itself, rather than a theory about it – just as the point of a great piece of music is just the music itself.

Evan: Maybe. And maybe we can get closer to the secret of the universe by looking more closely at the analogy of music.

Conversation 10:
The Music of the Spheres

Libby: But is the universe really music?

Is the universe music?

'Isa: The ancient Greeks certainly thought so. Pythagoras thought the universe was a large musical instrument, and the planets made perfect music, "the music of the spheres." The only reason we didn't hear it, he said, is because we're *in* it. In fact we *are* it, we are part of it. Our movements, our lives, are part of the cosmic movements, the "music of the spheres." We're "spheres" too.

`Libby: You said Plato spent more time on music than on politics in his *Republic*. Why? What's music got to do with politics?

'Isa: A lot. Damon of Athens said, "Let me write the songs of a nation and I care not who writes its laws." The *Republic* is about justice in the state, *and* justice in

Justice in states, souls, cosmos, and music

the soul, *and* justice in the cosmos, *and* justice in music. It's all the same concept: a kind of universal cosmic harmony or right order or "music" that both souls and states participate in.

Libby: So if we find our Theory of Everything, it's going to solve some problems in politics too?

Confucianism's successful harmonies

'Isa: Absolutely. That's what the ancient Chinese thought. Both the Taoists and the Confucians thought that. They both thought that understanding cosmic harmony was the key to political order and peace. And it worked. Confucianism was the most successful social system in the history of the world, if you measure it by longevity, by staying power, and by population, by the number of people who lived it.

The sound of silence vs. the music of the spheres

Evan: But we moderns don't hear "the music of the spheres" when we look up at the night sky any more. We hear "the sound of silence."

Libby: Why do you think that happened?

'Isa: I think it's because our inner ear became tone deaf. Our 'third eye' became blind.

Libby: And why did *that* happen?

'Isa: That's a long story, but the important point is not to trace it but to fix it. How can we restore the ear that hears this cosmic music?

Libby: I think you just mentioned one pretty good suggestion: Taoism. That cosmic music you're looking for – that's what Lao Tzu called the Tao, "the way," and what the Hindus called "Rta," and what the Iroquois called "Orenda." It's the way nature works, the way nature is. It's the very nature of nature. And it's also the way *we* should work and the way we should think if we're wise.

Tao, Rta, and Orenda

The nature of nature

'Isa: As a Muslim, I question that idea. Why should we imitate nature if we have God's own word revealed to us directly in the Qur'an? I thought you Christians believed you had God's own direct revelation too, in your New Testament and in Jesus. Don't you call both of them "the Word of God"?

Libby: Yeah, but we also believe God created nature, and designed it – as you do too – so the way nature works reflects the way God works. So this "way" isn't just the way of nature; it reflects the way of God, the very nature of God.

'Isa: But there's no God in Taoism.

God is Tao.

Libby: Sure there is. He's anonymous.

'Isa: What do you mean by that?

Libby: Lao Tzu didn't talk about God. He didn't know Tao was God. But he sure knew that God was Tao, he knew what Ultimate Reality was like.

'Isa: No he didn't. Because God isn't like anything. That's what the name "Michael" means, the name of the great archangel: "Who is like God?"

God is like nothing, everything is like God.

Evan: You're both right. God isn't like anything else, but everything else is like God because everything else is His creation, His art. Libby, how do you think Taoism is going to help us find the Theory of Everything?

Libby: You're looking for the universal music, right?

Evan: Yes.

Libby: You can hear that music in a lot of places, a lot of echoes in nature. It's like seeing light reflected off many different mirrors, but it's the same light. So it's the same music, the same theme. You know, the Bible of Taoism, the *Tao Te Ching,* is the third most popular book in the world, next to the Bible and the Qur'an. And it connects everything: it finds the same Tao in things as different as politics, and breathing, and women, *Where do we find Tao?* and water, and peace, and wild animals, and butchers cutting meat, and bowls, and windows.

'Isa: So what's the formula? Can you be a little more specific about what this "way of nature" is?

Libby: Sure. Two of its principles are Yin and Yang and Wei Wu Wei.

'Isa: I know Yin and Yang: the cos- *Yin and yang* mic feminine and masculine, right?

Libby: Yes. The universal polarity, the universal relativity of all things in nature.

'Isa: I'm instinctively suspicious of relativities.

Libby: Why? Don't you believe Allah is the only absolute?

'Isa: Hmm . . . you've got a good point there, Libby. But what is "Wei Wu Wei"?

Libby: It means literally "acting with- *Acting without acting* out acting," or "doing by not-doing." It's soul-surfing on the waves of nature instead of hot-dogging and competing. It's what Tao does. It's what water does. It's what surfers do when they become one with the water. *They* understand Tao, but they understand it intuitively, with the 'third eye.' Actually, they understand it kinesthetically. They feel it, in their bodies. No, I take that back, they feel it in their souls. No, I take that back again, they feel it in both. No, I take it back again, they feel it in the unity of the two. The body and the soul aren't separated any more when you're on a wave. And you and the water, you and the wave, you and the sea, you and nature – you're not separated any more either.

'Isa: I have to say I'm a little suspicious of that too, Libby. Do you mean you pass beyond individuality and free choice and responsibility?

Libby: No. You still make choices, with your body.

'Isa: But the material universe doesn't make choices, so you're not really one with the universe. Unless logic no longer makes sense. You are free, and nature is not free, therefore you are not nature.

Libby: You *are* nature. You are the part of nature that *is* free.

'Isa: So you're not denying freedom. You're not a pantheist, or a materialist, or even a naturalist.

Libby: Of course not. I wouldn't deny my own name. Liberty – that's who I am!

'Isa: And you don't think the water

Surfers as Taoists

This is not pantheism or paganism

is literally a god, with a will, like Poseidon, do you?

Libby: No.

'Isa: Then if you have free will and the wave doesn't, you're not simply one with the wave.

Libby: Of course not. I come into it from outside, and it spits me out again. But I *become* one with it for a moment. For that moment when I'm in it, I *am* one with it. Because I'm not "in" it as a sardine is in a can. The sardine isn't one with the can. It's more like mental telepathy, when you become one with another mind, you get "in" the other mind.

How are Surfers "in" the wave?

'Isa: But matter can't do that, only mind can. So mind and matter are really two different things. Matter is determined and spirit is free.

Libby: I'm not denying that. But there's got to be some common pattern, some common music to both of them. And part of that music is freedom. When I'm in a wave, I know, for sure, that I'm free. I'm freer there than anywhere else, and I'm also *surer* that I'm free there than anywhere else. But I also know for sure that I'm destined or fated.

The music common to mind and matter

'Isa: Detrmined?

Libby: "Fated," I'd say, not "determined." Dominoes are determined; people are fated.

'Isa: So you feel both more free and more fated at the same time.

Music as fate and freedom

Libby: Yes. Exactly like music! It's the freest of all the arts, the most "spiritual," and also the most necessary, the most determined, and the most mathematical.

'Isa: So if it's spirit that's free and matter that's determined, you must also feel more spiritual and more material at the same time in music and also in surfing.

More spiritual and more material at the same time

Libby: Yes, that's exactly right! More spiritual, yes. And more material. And at the same time, and even for the same reason, somehow.

'Isa: How can that be?

Libby: That's what Nicodemus said to Jesus about being born again.

'Isa: And what did Jesus answer?

Libby: "Try it, you'll like it."

Evan: That's a very loose translation.

Libby: He was a very loose kind of guy. Like Lao Tzu.

'Isa: I don't want to tame your looseness, Libby, but I have to try to understand it, and that means tightening it up, expressing it in ideas, translating this "right-brain" thing into "left-brain" categories. I'd like to try to understand this "Tao" by using one of the most commonsensical categories in the world: Aristotle's four causes, the idea we used to understand Jung's "synchronicity."

Libby: You listened to my looseness, so I guess I better listen to your tightness. Go ahead.

'Isa: We know the universe is one.

Libby: Wait a minute. We don't know that. Maybe God created other universes.

'Isa: That's not what I mean. Whether He did or not, this one is a *uni*-verse. It has a unity.

Did God create other universes?

Libby: Of course.

'Isa: And we know that that unity is intrinsic to it. It's more than an extrinsic unity. And what that means can be explained by the four causes. Two of the four causes are extrinsic to the effect and two are intrinsic. The intrinsic causes are the form and the matter, the formal cause and the material cause. The extrinsic causes are the origin and the end, the efficient cause and the final cause. So even if the unity of the universe is the Will of God as its efficient cause, and the glory of God as its final cause, it's also something

What kind of unity does the universe have?

else, it's an intrinsic unity. Just as Evan said before.

Libby: That makes sense. The artist puts a unity *into* his art.

'Isa: And that unity can't be merely the material unity, the fact that everything in the universe is made of matter, or energy. There's got to be a formal unity too, a common pattern, a common music. That's what we're looking for.

Libby: That would be something like the soul of the universe, right?

'Isa: Well, something like that. If our soul is the form and our body is the matter, that's an analogy, at least.

Libby: So it would be what the point is to the joke, or the meaning to the words.

'Isa: But what would it be to the music?

Libby: It would be the *music* of the music. It would answer the question: *what* music? *This* music. But the language of that answer would have to be music, not words. Nobody can say what a piece of music *means* in words. The music explains the words, the words don't explain the music. To understand the music, you just have to fall into the music, as you fall into the rhythm when you dance.

Falling into the music

{148}

10. The Music of the Spheres

Evan: I've often wondered about the relation between music and the cosmos. Why does some music seem different in kind, not just in degree, as if it's on another dimension, or from another world – as if it's echoes from the unfallen music of Eden? Why do we love certain harmonies and certain rhythms more than others? Are they closer to the great pattern of the cosmic music? Somebody should write about music and the Tao; the two seem so closely connected.

Echoes of Eden's music?

'Isa: I think some did. The ancient Greeks, for one. We've already mentioned Pythagoras and his "music of the spheres," and Plato, and the Stoics, with their "Logos."

Evan: We Christians believe the Logos became incarnate in Christ. So Christ *is* the Tao, the Cosmic Music.

Christ as the cosmic music

'Isa: But that can't be part of your universal theory, because belief in Christ isn't universal. Only one third of the people in the world share it. A Theory of Everything can't be religion-specific.

Evan: We believe Christ is *not* religion-specific. We believe He is God.

'Isa: But most people don't. So *their* "Logos" is not Christ.

The universality of *logos*

{149}

Evan: No, that doesn't follow. Your own Qur'an says that all who surrender to Allah, even if they're Jews or Christians or even pagans, are Muslims, "surrenderers."

Libby: A Muslim is like a rose then.

'Isa: Like a rose?

Libby: "A rose by any other name would smell as sweet."

Evan: We don't need to settle the religious issue to find the Theory of Everything. We don't even need to raise it. Because we have only one real universe, and only one God. When Lao Tzu intuited his Tao, that wasn't *his* Tao, that was *the* Tao, and if what he said was true, it was true of the real nature of Allah, or Jesus, or Brahman, or the absolute. There *is* only one God, you know, no matter how many names we invent for Him. Or have you forgotten that?

'Isa: *I* haven't.

Evan: So let's look at more versions of the one cosmic music.

Libby: Right. Let's gather our data from all the different versions.

Evan: No "versions" don't amount to *data*, they're just *theories*. But it's good to canvass theories, especially if they all have something striking in common.

'Isa: Cassiodorus is another source. Cassiodorus
He said the universe is governed by
music.

Evan: Who's he?

'Isa: A Latin Christian in the Dark Governing China by music
Ages. And then there's the ancient
Chinese emperor – I forget which one –
who governed the world's largest empire
by music. He walked disguised through
the main cities of China listening to the
music his citizens played and sang. If it
was in harmony with the Tao, he left the
city alone, but if it wasn't, he sent soldiers
there because he knew trouble would
break out soon. And it worked. It worked!
It's not just a fairy tale.

Libby: I think most other cultures
understand that. There are African versions of it too. We're the only culture
that's forgotten it – and we dare to think
of ourselves as superior. "We are the people, and wisdom will die with us."

Evan: What about history? Does the
Tao, or the Logos, structure history as
well as nature? Human life as well as the
life of the universe?

'Isa: It has to, if it's universal. But it
would have to do that differently, because
man is different. I think the pagans didn't

really appreciate that point; only the Jews, the Christians, and the Muslims did.

Evan: Appreciate what point?

'Isa: Two points, and they seem opposite. First, that there's a single Tao for both nature and history, and so history too can make sense, make *logos*. And second, that human history is very different from nature because man is very different from nature, because he's free.

One Tao for both nature and history, yet history transcends nature

Evan: Let's look at those two things one at a time.

'Isa: Good. The first one is how history can be a science. The ancient Greeks never developed history as a science or a philosophy. Only Jews, Christians, and Muslims came up with a philosophy of history, based on their scriptures. That's partly because of our belief in creation and the Day of Judgment, an absolute beginning and an absolute ending to time. The story of the universe, like the story of human life, is a meaningful story because it has a beginning, a middle, and an end. There can be a Logos to it. The Greek Logos governs nature, but not history. The Greeks had plenty of cosmologies, but no philosophy of history. Augustine's was the first one – *The City of God* – and that was based on the Bible.

Why history was not a science for the Greeks

{152}

Libby: But the Chinese didn't limit the Tao that way, as the Greeks did. In the *Tao Te Ching*, the Tao governs – or can govern, if we let it – human life just as it governs nature.

'Isa: That's true.

Evan: What about the history of the second idea, that man is radically different from nature because he has free will?

'Isa: The pagans never quite came up with the idea of human free will and the primacy of individual moral responsibility, though Aristotle came close. That idea came mainly from the prophets, Jewish and Christian and Muslim.

The origin of the idea of free will

Libby: Why is this history lesson important? Aren't we going off on a tangent?

Evan: We are. But if we find the Theory of Everything, it will have to account for history as well as nature, *and* their unity, *and* the difference between them.

Libby: How?

Evan: I think we need another whole day for that question, OK?

Libby: OK. What about using the clue of music by actually listening to actual musicians and great composers?

Sibelius, the composer of logos

Evan: Yes, let's do that too. Especially the ones who believed that music was cosmic. Sibelius, for instance. He wrote that his music "was brought to life by the Logos," and he described his Fifth Symphony this way: " – as if God the Father had thrown down pieces of mosaic from Heaven's floor and asked me to solve how the picture once looked." That, it seems to me, is exactly what we're trying to do here.

'Isa: We've been talking *about* doing it so much that we've ignored *doing* it.

Evan: You don't just "do it." It takes thousands of hours, maybe thousands of conversations.

'Isa: But you have to start somewhere.

Evan: We did that. We started.

'Isa: With what?

Evan: With music.

'Isa: So let's continue with music.

Evan: But let's be specific. What are some of the connections between music and the universe?

'Isa: What connections do *you* see?

Buddha's diamond

Evan: One of them is obviously rhythm. Everything in the universe has rhythm: a beginning and an ending. Buddha called that "the pure and spotless

{154}

eye of the *dharma*," in his "Diamond sutra": the doctrine that "whatever is an arising thing, that is also a ceasing thing."

'Isa: But he was wrong. He forgot us. He forgot the immortality of the soul.

Libby: And the resurrection of the body.

'Isa: True, but for everything else he was right. Everything *in time,* at least, has rhythm, beginnings and endings, except for the one thing in time that's destined for eternity: us.

The diamond shattered

Evan: *What* rhythm? Let's be still more specific.

'Isa: The most basic rhythm is the coming-forth and the return. Everything comes from the Creator's will as the first efficient cause; and everything seeks, and moves toward, and returns to, the Creator as its final cause, its end and purpose.

The rhythm of exit and return: the Big Bang

Evan: So the whole universe, from the Big Bang to the Last Judgment, is a gigantic wave, a wave of creation that bursts forth into all finite beings, and then draws all beings back to itself.

The universe as one great wave

'Isa: And the flotsam and jetsam on that wave is everything in the universe: all people and animals and plants and minerals and atoms and particles and planets and galaxies and black holes and antimatter – everything.

Everything surfs!

Libby: Hey, that's cool. If the universe is a big wave, then everything surfs!

'Isa: Yes, on the rhythm of the wave, and also on the little waves that are ripples of that big wave.

Evan: And here's a second specific link between music and the universe: tonality.

Tonality waves

Libby: That make waves too, doesn't it?

Evan: Yes.

Libby: How?

Evan: Think of it as a fabric. Its vertical warp is harmony, and its horizontal woof is melody, and together they make the wave pattern.

Psychological waves

Libby: I look at a wave more in terms of psychological dynamics. A wave is conflict and resolution.

'Isa: So is music.

History waves

Evan: And so is history.

'Isa: In fact, whatever it's made of, whether it's water or the energy of the Big Bang or psychological dynamics between people, a wave is always essentially rhythm. And rhythm is simply order in time, *logos* in time.

Evan: That's the Incarnation!

'Isa: No . . . that's partisan theology. That's not the universal essence of rhythm.

Libby: Isn't the essence of rhythm the *beat*?

Evan: No, it isn't. Chant has rhythm but no beat.

Libby: Is that really music, then?

Evan: I'd ask the opposite question at the other end of the spectrum: is rap, or even hard rock, really music, if it's almost all beat?

Libby: You're not into today's sounds, are you?

Evan: No. It sounds to me as infernal as chant sounds angelic.

'Isa: Now we're doing partisan aesthetics!

Evan: Back to science, then. Rhythm is universal because when you look at anything real, you can always find its rhythm, its wave pattern. Science itself is based on this rhythm. Because a scientist always looks for patterns of behavior in nature, ordered recurrences. That's what a formula summarizes.

Libby: And psychologists and sociologists and anthropologists look for the very same thing in *human* behavior.

Evolution
as a wave

Evan: Scientific laws always describe these rhythmic patterns.

'Isa: But there are fundamentally different kinds of rhythms in nature, aren't there? There's one kind of rhythm in puppies becoming dogs and then dogs having puppies, kittens becoming cats and cats having kittens. And then there's another, larger pattern in the long-range evolution of dogs and cats as *species*. And a still larger pattern in the expansion of the universe ever since the Big Bang. But all of these processes have the same form: the form of the wave.

Evan: That's right, 'Isa, but that's all well known. In fact, almost everything we've said so far is pretty well known. We're looking for the key to the unknown, to a new Universal Wave Theory.

'Isa: But the key to the unknown is probably something known. I don't think we're looking for some specific thing that's unknown when we look for a "Theory of Everything," but more like a new way of looking at the familiar, a new way of seeing it all together.

Libby: And how do you find that? How does that happen? How do people suddenly see something that was in front of them to begin with?

'Isa: How *do* they? You're the psychologist.

Libby: It doesn't always happen when they see new objects, but when they get into a different state of consciousness. When the adrenaline kicks in. When they get emotional. When something is threatened. When they hit a wall, or a cliff, or a crisis.

How to see the familiar

Crises open eyes

Evan: Well, then, maybe we're in a good position to find the Theory of Everything, because our whole culture and history and identity and meaning are in crisis.

'Isa: Then that's the next thing to talk about.

Conversation 11:
Cultural Consequences

Libby: Everybody knows the psychological principle involved here: we appreciate a thing only by contrast, and that's why we appreciate somebody only when they die, or go away, or when their life is threatened.

Evan: That works for music too.

Libby: How? Music isn't dead.

Schoenberg as music's murderer

Evan: In Schoenberg it is. He's the arch-modernist, the musical deconstructionist. For Schoenberg, tonality was dead because Logos is dead, and Logos is dead because God is dead.

'Isa: Was it explicitly religious for him?

Evan: Yes, it was. His basic slogan for musical creativity was this: "Nothing constrains me."

'Isa: I understand. That's blasphemous.

Libby: I *don't* understand. How is that "blasphemous"?

'Isa: That's exactly the philosophy of Satan.

The philosophy of Satan

Evan: When he rebelled against God's order and God's law, and brought into existence evil for the first time. I know no other artist whose central credo is such a perfect example of pure evil, evil incarnate. His disciple John Cage went so far as to *forbid* harmony.

John Cage vs. harmony

'Isa: I think that's what they do that in Hell. They forbid harmony.

Evan: Cage banished the inner laws of music from music.

Libby: He's the guy who used vacuum cleaners as the instruments in his symphony orchestra, right?

Evan: Right.

Libby: He must have hated music. How come he was a musician?

Evan: He hated *real* music. He simply hated reality; he hated everything real.

'Isa: Like Marx. Marx wrote somewhere, "Everything that exists deserves to perish."

The deathwish

Libby: That's a deathwish. Like the Nazis had.

Evan: And Schoenberg's disciples, just like Hitler's, called him "Savior."

Libby: What did they think he saved them from?

Salvation from logos into chaos

Evan: From logos.

Libby: Into what?

Evan: Into chaos. He cultivated chaos, he hated order, reason, law, harmony, beauty, justice, and intelligibility. In other words, he hated music. So naturally, he went into music. To kill it.

Libby: Why focus on one weirdo? He's not all of modern music.

Dali and Picasso vs. logos

Evan: Because his philosophy – which I've labeled the philosophy of Hell – has dominated mainline modern music, and art too, in a lot of less explicit and less extreme forms. Salvatore Dali, for instance. He said, "The goal of my work is to systematize confusion and to disorder reality." And Picasso. He deliberately disfigured the human face.

'Isa: Why is that so important?

The centrality of the face

Evan: Because the human face is the most sacred and spiritual matter in the universe, the most beautiful thing in the universe. That's what he focused his attack on.

Libby: Wait a minute. Didn't he do

"Guernica," that idealistic anti-war protest painting? That was a moral protest against war and destruction, wasn't it?

Evan: No, it wasn't. It wasn't a moral protest against abnormality in the name of the normal or the norm. It was a normalization of abnormality. It was an artistic glorification of disorder. Not of war itself, but of disorder. All his pictures do that.

The normalization of abnormality

'Isa: Your whole society glorifies disorder: sexual disorder. "Nothing constrains me" – that's everybody's attitude to sex in your society, even if it isn't everybody's attitude to art. So it's no surprise to me that your society also glorifies musical disorder and artistic disorder. I think it's a kind of rationalization of sexual disorder. And drugs and alcohol: that's a third kind of disorder, intellectual disorder, scrambling your brains. I think all three revolutions have the same pattern: the anti-music pattern, the anti-rhythm pattern, the anti-logos pattern. The sexual revolution attacks logos in the body, and the musical revolution attacks logos in the soul, the heart, the imagination. And the drug revolution attacks logos in the mind.

Sexual disorder and musical disorder

Libby: Don't be so down on us, 'Isa.

Surfing as the counter-revolution

Because surfing is the antidote to all three of those revolutions, and that also comes from our culture.

'Isa: All three revolutions? How?

Libby: Because no drug is higher than the high you get on a wave. And nothing is more perfect music than a wave. And nothing is more sexy than a wave.

'Isa: Well, I guess there's just nothing more to say, then. You've found the Theory of Everything. Thanks, Libby. Even if the rest of the world won't call you the Über-Einstein, we will.

Surfboards as medicines

Libby: I didn't claim I've found the Theory, but I do think I've found the vehicle to get there. It's right here in my room. It's red, and it's got a leash attached.

And even if you can't *think* it, even if you can't get Everything into your head as a theory, you can still *do* it.

'Isa: Do what?

Libby: Heal the three deepest diseases in the culture at once.

'Isa. Are you also selling the Brooklyn Bridge?

Libby: Just try it. You'll like it.

'Isa: But the Theory of Everything is like reading the Mind of God. Are you telling me that you get into the Mind of God by a surfboard?

Libby: The board's nothing. You can do it without a board. You can just body-surf. But yes, getting into a wave is getting into the Mind of God, because a wave is the Mind of God. That's why surfers have that dazed look outside the water. They've been in heaven, they've seen the light. They've been inside the sacred cathedral, inside the cosmic dance. They call it "the Green Room" or "the Green Cathedral." As they say about the tube of a wave, "God is in the tube."

A wave as the mind of God

'Isa: Sounds like a mystical experience.

Libby: It is. It's like the classic near-death-experience or out-of-body experience. You're plunged into a dark tunnel, and drawn to a light at the far end. Like the birth canal. And time itself changes. It becomes elastic. Every second lasts forever. And it's not just poets and mystics who say this: ordinary, pragmatic surfers feel that way, and to explain it they often find their way to words that they never speak about anything else: mystical words, poetic words, cosmic words, even blends of these with scientific words. For instance,

Being born, dying, and "the Green Room"

one calls it "a wash in the space-time continuum."

'Isa: I'm skeptical. How can something as materialistic as surfing put you
into the Mind of God?

Libby: It's not materialistic. It's material. Surfers are not money grubbers.
They're poor and happy. But they're
kinesthetic, not abstract. Because that's
how God heals us: through matter, especially through water.

*How God
heals us
through
water*

'Isa: Why water?

Libby: We should have another conversation about that.

Evan: You two go ahead for a while.
I'd like to listen.

Conversation 12: Water Magic

'Isa: OK, so what have you learned about water from your surfing that scientists don't know about it from their experiments, Libby?

Libby: How it heals us.

'Isa: We all know it feels good. Is that all you mean by "how it heals us"?

Libby: No. It's more than just a temporary good feeling, like when you take a bath. Surfing isn't just big bathing. You don't become one with your bathtub, or the ripples in your bathtub, but you become one with the sea, and with the wave. And that heals you because it opens the pores of your soul – not just your body – and lets the universe in. It overcomes Overcoming epidermiolatry.

'Isa: What's epidermiolatry? I never heard that word.

Libby: I made it up. It means idolatry

of the epidermis, answering the profound question "who am I?" by saying "I'm everything inside my epidermis, I'm a brain in a skin bag."

'Isa: We already refuted materialism.

Libby: I don't mean just materialism. I mean egotism.

'Isa: Nobody defends egotism. Every ethical system in the world condemns it.

Libby: I don't mean just ethical egotism. I mean psychological egotism: confusing yourself with your ego.

'Isa: But "ego" *means* "self," or "I." To say that I equals I isn't "confusion." It's called "identity."

Libby: But there's more in yourself than your I, just as there's more in your face than your eyes.

'Isa: The unconscious, you mean? The "right brain" stuff?

Libby: No, even more than that. The whole universe.

'Isa: I don't understand what you mean.

Libby: I'll try to help you understand. Look between your shoulders. What do you see?

'Isa: My head.

Libby: No, you don't. You only see your head if you look at a mirror. Try again.

'Isa: What do you mean, "try again?"

Libby: I mean, "try again." Take it literally, O great philosopher. Open your eyes and tell me what you see between your shoulders.

'Isa: Nothing. I can't see between my shoulders.

Libby: But you can! You're doing it right now.

'Isa: *What* am I seeing?

Libby: You're seeing *me*. And this room, and this house, and this world, and this universe. The whole crazy universe is there between your shoulders and you don't notice it!

Not your head but the universe

'Isa: The subject that sees the universe is there, yes. But not the object seen. The object is out there.

Libby: But it's also in here. That's why you can see it. It's in two places. It bilocates. And you're in two places too: you put yourself out there into the universe when you see it.

The universe bilocates.

'Isa: OK, suppose I admit the truth of your metaphysical epistemology; what does that have to do with water, or surfing, or the Theory of Everything?

Libby: Before you have a Theory of Everything you have to have data, right?

'Isa: Right.

Libby: And the data for a Theory of Everything has to be "everything-data" in some way, doesn't it?

'Isa: In some way, yes.

Self = open to the whole universe

Libby: Well, that's the first way to get "everything data," that's the way we all have right there at the beginning of our thinking. I am open to the whole universe.

'Isa: I guess I follow you. But I don't see why that's so profound or important.

Libby: If you surfed, you would see it.

'Isa: How?

Libby: You'd get out of your epidermis then.

Is surfing a mystical experience?

'Isa: Do you mean to claim that surfing is a mystical experience? And do you mean to claim that you have to have mystical experience or else you'll never find the Theory of Everything?

Libby: I don't know the answer to either of those two questions. Do you?

'Isa: No, not really.

Libby: All right, then, keep yourself open. Like the sun.

'Isa: What do you mean, "like the sun"?

Libby: It's like the poet Hafiz says: "Even after all this time, the sun never says to the earth – 'you owe me.' Look what happens with a love like that. It lights the whole sky." The wisdom of the sun

'Isa: That's a great Sufi quote.

Libby: So you *do* get it.

'Isa: I do get it. So how does water fit in, then?

Libby: Like I said, it heals your spirit.

'Isa: *How?*

Libby: This is my point, exactly: how water works to solve the *problem* in all problems. We all have problems, right?

'Isa: Of course. But they're all different: sin, selfishness, stupidity, death, disease, destruction, pain, poverty, pettiness, war, weakness, weariness of spirit . . . Many problems

Libby: Enough, already, you professional pessimist. Now all those problems – all problems – founder on one fact.

'Isa: Just one? What fact? = One problem

Libby: What do you think? Why can't we just solve them all? Why can't we solve any of them?

'Isa: Because we don't surrender.

Libby: You're right – although I think you mean something different than I do by "surrender." You mean "islam," don't you? Surrender to the Will of Allah?

'Isa: Yes.

Libby: I mean something broader than that. I mean surrender as such, surrender as a psychological principle.

'Isa: Giving up to anyone but Allah isn't conquering your problems. It's letting them conquer you.

Libby: You don't understand. Just listen a minute, will you?

'Isa: OK.

Evan: *I've* been listening for ten minutes now, and I'm wondering how this is going to help us find the Theory of Everything. Are you getting closer to that, Libby, or are you wandering farther away on a surfari?

Libby: I'm getting to the very heart of that, Evan. I'm getting to how water gets to the heart of it.

Evan: OK, I'm listening.

Libby: All our problems founder on the Bootstraps Principle.

'Isa: What's that?

Libby: You can't lift yourself up by your own bootstraps.

'Isa: I never saw bootstraps.

Libby: Neither did I. But you can

Surrender as a psychological principle

The Bootstraps Principle

{172}

imagine what they are, right? And you can imagine how natural it is to believe that you can lift yourself up by pulling up on them, right? And then when you try it, it just doesn't work.

Evan: Because of Newtonian mechanics. Because to every action there is an equal and opposite reaction.

Libby: Whatever. So you see where I'm going with this, right?

'Isa: Yes. All our problems are *our* problems. We can solve only "out there" problems, not "in here" problems.

Libby: Exactly. So how *do* those problems get solved? Because sometimes they do!

How do any problems get solved?

'Isa: God. If there were no God, there would be no one to lift us up, and we'd just be tugging at our own bootstraps forever.

Libby: That's true. But how does God do it?

'Isa: We don't know. We can't know. We're not God – we have to keep reminding ourselves of that! – so we can't understand God's spiritual technology.

Libby: Yes we can. We can see it. We can experience it.

'Isa: What is it, then?

God as a
tide lifting
our boats

Libby: He heals us by matter, by energy, by the universe. He lifts us up like a
tide lifting up a boat. Because we're floating on His water world all the time.

'Isa: That's a nice metaphor, but
what exactly does it mean?

Healing
spirit by
matter

Libby: It means that He heals our
spirits by matter, and especially water.

'Isa: You say that because you're a
Christian, and you're thinking of the Incarnation and the Crucifixion, and Baptism.

Libby: Yes, I am; but I'm also thinking
of all the rest of the matter in the universe, not just the matter inside Jesus's
epidermis. And I'm thinking of all the
water in our water world, not just the
water used in baptisms. Water is global, so
it washes everybody. "He makes His rain
fall on the just and on the unjust."

'Isa: That's true. But how does that
get us any nearer to the Theory of
Everything?

Evan: That's what I'm still wondering.

Earth *and*
Humanity
are 70%
water

Libby: Just a little more patience, guys,
OK? I'm almost there. Water is global
within as well as without. Our bodies are
70 percent water. We almost *are* water.
Our planet is also 70 percent water – the
same proportion. Coincidence? No way.

12. Water Magic

Evan: When we're first conceived, we're *more* than 70 percent water.

Libby: And when we die, we become *less* than 70 percent water, we get dehydrated. So, you see, water is the secret of life. So the more you become one with water, the closer you are to the secret of life. That's why surfers always say they "get inside" – not just inside a wave but inside the secret of life, inside water itself. Not just with their bodies, but with their minds.

Water as the secret of life

Evan: You've got water on the brain.

Libby: No, on the mind. Remember that distinction.

Evan: Of course. I was making a lame joke.

'Isa: Seriously, the very first saying from the very first philosopher in history, Thales of Miletus, was that "everything is water." Maybe that will be the last word too.

Thales as the *last* philosopher

Evan: St. Teresa of Avila said she learned more from water than from books.

St. Theresa on water

Libby: I'm not St. Teresa, but I'll second that. I get bored with books after a while. In fact, I get bored with everything after a while: with everything except

Water heals boredom

Everything. And water is a natural icon of Everything, so I guess that's why I don't get bored with water. I have A.D.D., you know. But I just never get bored with moving water. I can play in waves forever.

'Isa: And what do you think is the significance of that, Libby?

Libby: I think that's a foretaste of Heaven.

'Isa: You mean you think you're going to play in God forever? Are you going to surf in God?

Heaven = Surfing in God

Libby: Yeah, that's it. In fact, that's just about the best description of Heaven I've ever heard.

Evan: So how does that help you find the Theory of Everything?

Play vs. theory

Libby: I guess that means I'd rather *play* in Everything than have a theory of it. Does that disappoint you, Evan?

Evan: One part of me says yes. Another part of me says no.

Libby: And why isn't your second self disappointed?

Evan: Because it would rather have a healing than a theory.

Libby: And which self do you think is wiser?